BERTRAM

FLETCHER ROBINSON

A FOOTNOTE TO

THE HOUND OF THE BASKERVILLES

By

I0160967

Brian W. Pugh
&
Paul R. Spiring

BERTRAM FLETCHER ROBINSON

First published in 2008
© Copyright 2008
Brian W Pugh and Paul R Spiring

The right of Brian W Pugh and Paul R Spiring to be identified as the authors of this work has been asserted by them in accordance with the Copyright, Designs and Patents Act 1998. All rights reserved. No reproduction, copy or transmission of this publication may be made without written permission. No paragraph of this publication may be reproduced, copied or transmitted save with the written permission or in accordance with the provisions of the Copyright Act 1956 (as amended). Any person who does any unauthorised act in relation to this publication may be liable to criminal prosecution and civil claims for damage.

ISBN-9781904312406

MX Publishing Ltd, 335 Princess Park Manor, Royal Drive, London, N11 3GX
www.mxpublishing.co.uk

Dedication

The authors dedicate this book to the memory of Richard Lancelyn Green (see Plate 1). He was widely regarded as the foremost expert on both Arthur Conan Doyle and Sherlock Holmes, at the time of his death.

Plate 1. Richard Lancelyn Green,
(10th July 1953 – 27th March 2004).
COURTESY OF JUNE LANCELYN GREEN

Foreword

Millions of people, the world over, owe a debt of gratitude to Bertram Fletcher Robinson. The author, Arthur Conan Doyle, insisted that every first edition of *The Hound of the Baskervilles* carried an acknowledgement to his assistance with that novel. The seeds for the story were sown when Fletcher Robinson told Conan Doyle tales about ghostly hounds and the bleak wilderness of Dartmoor. But how many readers are actually aware of just who Fletcher Robinson was?

During 1900, Bertram Fletcher Robinson was covering the South African War for the *Daily Express*, whilst Arthur Conan Doyle was also there serving as a volunteer surgeon at The Langman Field Hospital — and gathering material for his eventual history *The Great Boer War*. Fletcher Robinson was primarily a journalist, with the good journalist's versatility and wide range of interests (attributes that Conan Doyle shared). Before his early death, he edited *The Granta*, *The Isthmian Library*, *Daily Express*, *Vanity Fair* and *The World*.

His books are rather neglected, which is a pity, because there is much of interest in them. His love of sport is evident in *Rugby Football, Football, Rowing & Punting* and *Sporting Pictures*. The title of *Britain's Sea-Kings and Sea-Fights* explains itself.

BERTRAM FLETCHER ROBINSON

Then there is the fiction. He wrote over fifty short stories including two serialisations that were both compiled and published as novels; *The Trail of the Dead* (with J. Malcolm Fraser), and more famously, *The Chronicles of Addington Peace*. As you might guess, both books are detective stories and each is now highly collectable.

Roger Johnson,
Editor: *The Sherlock Holmes Journal*.

Plate 2. *The Hound of the Baskervilles* as
drawn by Sidney Paget for *The Strand Magazine*.

Preface

Between 1887 and 1893, Arthur Conan Doyle wrote 2 novellas and 24 short stories that each featured his legendary detective, Sherlock Holmes. However, by November 1891, Conan Doyle had grown weary of this character and remarked in a letter to his mother that he was contemplating 'slaying Holmes in the last and winding him up for good and all'.

In December 1893, Conan Doyle 'killed-off' Holmes at the Reichenbach Falls in Switzerland in a story entitled *The Final Problem* that was published by *The Strand Magazine*. The news of his death was greeted with dismay by many and Conan Doyle was subsequently besieged with letters of protest!

In 1901, Conan Doyle 'resurrected' Holmes for his novella, *The Hound of the Baskervilles* (set during 1889). This story was an unprecedented success and it was followed up with a further 32 short stories and 1 novella that each feature Holmes (1903-1927). However, none of these stories surpassed the popular success of *The Hound of the Baskervilles*. Since its publication, it has formed the basis for no fewer than 19 full-length films in six different languages.

The Hound of the Baskervilles (see Plate 2) first appeared as a serialisation in both the British and American editions of *The Strand Magazine* (1901/1902). During 1902, George Newnes, the publisher of that magazine, also produced a British and American book edition. In all four cases, there is a printed acknowledgement to the help and assistance that was provided by Bertram Fletcher Robinson.

Since that time, much has been written about the extent of Fletcher Robinson's involvement with the story. However, much of this is conjecture because he died less than 5 years after the publication of the final serialized episodes and first book editions. During April 1961, Peter Ruber, the then editor of the *The Baker Street Gasogene*, wrote of Bertram Fletcher Robinson:

> ...one knows so little of this man that it is curious that no one has yet had the compulsion to search the library shelves and newspaper morgues concerning the mysterious circumstances surrounding his life, and of the even more mysterious circumstances surrounding his death...

This book was written in response to that invitation. The authors hope that by further illuminating the life and work of Fletcher Robinson, it might be better understood why Conan Doyle, a successful 42 year-old writer, should have chosen a seemingly unknown 30 year-old journalist, to assist him with what transpired to be his most famous literary legacy.

Brian W Pugh & Paul R Spiring
The Conan Doyle (Crowborough) Establishment.

Acknowledgements

The authors would like to thank the following for their assistance with this book; Ashburton Library (Devon), Phillip G. Bergem (Norwegian Explorers), Peter E. Blau, Michael Bourne (Baskerville family), Isla Brownless (Lambrook School), Cambridge University Library (Rare Books and Periodicals), Hugh Cooke (European School of Karlsruhe), Graeme de Bracey Marrs (Robinson family), Devon Record Office, Dimitry Demeersman (BFRonline.BIZ), Alistair Duncan (Author of *Eliminate the Impossible*), Shelah Duncan (The British Library), Simon Eliot (Headmaster of Sherborne School), Exeter Central Library (Westcountry Studies), Michael Freeland (Harold Michelmore & Company Solicitors, Newton Abbot), Laxmi Gadher (Record Copying Department of The National Archive, Richmond), General Register Office, John Genova, Stewart Gillies (The British Library), Annabel Gordon (TopFoto), Andrew Gough (The British Library), June Lancelyn Green, Freda Howlett (President of The Sherlock Holmes Society of London), Roger Johnson (Editor of *The Sherlock Holmes Journal*), Tim Johnson (The Sherlock Holmes Collection, The University of Minnesota), Liverpool Central Library and Archive, Ian MacGregor (Archive Information Manager for the Met Office, Exeter), Janice McNabb, Meade-King, Robinson and Company Limited (Liverpool), Chris Munt, National Portrait Gallery (London), Newton Abbot Library (Local Studies and Railway Studies), Peggy Perdue (The Friends of the Arthur Conan Doyle Collection, Toronto Public Library, Canada), Plymouth and West Devon Record Office, Plymouth Central Library (Local and Naval

BERTRAM FLETCHER ROBINSON

Studies), Mark Pool (Torquay Library), Christopher Redmond, John Richardson (Headmaster of Cheltenham College), Arthur Robinson (Robinson family), Jörg Rosenbruch (European School of Karlsruhe), Kay Rumford, Su Rumford, State Library of South Australia (Adelaide), Mark Steed (Headmaster of Kelly College, Tavistock), Totnes Library (Devon), Frances Willmoth (Archivist at Jesus College, Cambridge University), Doug Wrigglesworth (The Friends of the Arthur Conan Doyle Collection, Toronto Public Library, Canada) and especially both Patrick Casey (Clifton Rugby Club) and Philip Weller (The Baskerville Hounds [The Dartmoor Sherlock Holmes Study Group] and The Conan Doyle Study Group).

Contents

Chapter 1

Family and Early Childhood

Bertram Fletcher Robinson (hereafter BFR) was born on 22nd August 1870 at 80 Rose Lane, Mossley Vale, Wavertree, West Derby, Lancashire (later incorporated into the city of Liverpool and the county of Merseyside). He was the son of 43 year-old Joseph Fletcher Robinson (see Plate 3) and his second wife, 29 year-old Emily Robinson (née Hobson). Neither parent had any other children.

BFR's paternal great-grandfather, The Revd Thomas Robinson, was an independent minister at Hallford in Lancashire. His paternal grandfather, Richard Robinson, was born there on 10th July 1797 and received his education at the nearby Blackburn Academy. By 1823, Richard had also been ordained. He was then assigned to an independent ministry at Witham in Essex and lived there in a house called Ivy Chimneys.

Around 1825, The Revd Richard Robinson married Sarah Green Dennant (BFR's paternal grandmother). She was the daughter of The Revd John Dennant of Halesworth in Suffolk (BFR's maternal great grand-father). During the course of the next 14 years, the couple had 9 children (BFR's paternal aunts and uncles). These included: Sarah (b. 1826), Joseph Fletcher (1827-1903), John (1828-1913), Frederick (1832-1921), Ellen (b. 1834) and Hephzibah (b. 1837). The remaining children died from consumption in infancy.

1

BERTRAM FLETCHER ROBINSON

Plate 3. Joseph Fletcher Robinson (circa 1880).
COURTESY OF MEADE-KING, ROBINSON & CO. LTD.

Joseph Fletcher Robinson was namesake to The Revd Joseph Fletcher who had taught Richard Robinson at Blackburn Academy. Autobiographical notes written by Joseph's youngest brother, Frederick, report that theirs was a strictly religious upbringing. He and his siblings were obliged to attend chapel twice every Sunday and were prohibited from reading anything other than scripture.

During 1835, Joseph was enrolled as a weekly boarder at a small independent school at nearby Kelvedon. During 1838, his mother died and it fell upon Joseph's father to raise the 6 surviving children. Understandably, The Revd

BERTRAM FLETCHER ROBINSON

Richard Robinson needed some assistance and so he employed a young nurse called Caroline Boulton. However, this led to financial hardship and Joseph was compelled to seek employment in order to help support his family. During 1840, 13 year-old Joseph left home and was employed as an apprentice miller at Langley Mill, Great Waltham, Essex (some 12 miles from Witham).

During 1841, The Revd Richard Robinson remarried a 44 year-old widow called Elizabeth Wade from Colchester in Essex (BFR's paternal step grandmother). Frederick later recorded that this event triggered 'problems between him and some of his older children.' Two years later, Joseph contracted smallpox and returned to Ivy Chimneys to be nursed. This resulted in father and son reconciling their differences.

In 1848, The Revd Richard Robinson was offered a ministry at Hallfold and resigned his pastorate at Witham after some 25 years of service. He then relocated with his wife and two youngest daughters to the very same house in which he was born, 55 Hallfold, Whitworth, Rochdale, Manchester, Lancashire. About that same time, 21 year-old Joseph was employed as a 'commercial traveller' by a wholesale druggist called Robert Sumner of 9 Cable Street, Liverpool, Lancashire.

Between 1848 and 1850, Joseph visited South America and befriended Giuseppe Garibaldi. The two men fought together against the Argentinean dictator, Juan Manuel de Rosas in the Guerra Grande ('Great War'). Joseph's obituaries report that he was 'wounded three times' before

3

the conflict was eventually resolved during 1851 by an Anglo-French intervention.

During the Summer of 1850, 23 year-old Joseph Fletcher Robinson married 26 year-old Rosalinda Williams (affectionately referred to as 'Rosa') in Liverpool. Thereafter, the newly-weds set-up home at 33 Mount Pleasant, Liverpool. Rosa was the daughter of a retired London-based solicitor called George Edward Williams, originally from Oakham in Rutlandshire. During the course of the next 7 years, Joseph revisited South America several times and helped to map the west coast. On one occasion, he rode a horse 700 miles between Buenos Aires in Argentina and Santiago in Chile via The Andes mountain range, a feat that was then considered remarkable. It seems likely that Joseph later recounted such adventures to BFR and that this prompted BFR's passion for storytelling.

Around 1858, Joseph and Rosa relocated to 21 Chatsworth Street, Edge Hill, Liverpool. Shortly thereafter the couple moved again to nearby 5 Bagot Street, Wavertree, West Derby, Lancashire. The pair began attending services at an independent chapel in Renshaw Street and Joseph was soon elected a council member. On 21st June 1858, Joseph's 60 year-old father, The Revd Richard Robinson, died from 'pleurisy' and was buried at Hallfold Chapel, Whitworth, Rochdale. Joseph attended his father's funeral together with his brother, John (see Plate 4). Thereafter, Elizabeth Robinson, resided with her stepson, Joseph and Rosa at Bagot Street.

Plate 4. Sir John Robinson.
COURTESY OF THE TOPFOTO COLLECTION.

Plate 5. Richard Robinson.
COURTESY OF MEADE-KING, ROBINSON & CO. LTD.

During 1861, Joseph and Rosa were still residing at 5 Bagot Street with 64 year-old Elizabeth Robinson, 69 year-old George Williams (Joseph's widowed father-in-law), 7 year-old Louisa Robinson (Joseph's niece), 9 year-old Emily Lodge (visitor) and 25 year-old Margaret Jones (servant). Joseph was then employed as a 'wholesale druggist' by Robert Sumner.

During 1865, Joseph's 11 year-old nephew, Richard Robinson (see Plate 5), came to live at 5 Bagot Street. He had been enrolled as a day boy at the nearby Liverpool Collegiate Institute. Richard was the son of Joseph's youngest brother, Frederick Robinson, who was by then an 'ironmonger and journeyman' from Stowupland, Stowmarket, Suffolk. Later, Frederick became a churchwarden, chairman of his local parish council and a justice-of-the peace.

By 1866, Joseph had resigned his position as a 'wholesale druggist and drug grinder' with Robert Sumner & Company of 50a Lord Street and 45 Cable Street, Liverpool. Joseph then founded a business called *Joseph Robinson & Company* that traded-in molasses, oil and kerosene. He operated from premises located at 9 Orange Court, 85a Castle Street, Liverpool, and also from a warehouse situated in Bagot Street. This company still trades, under the name of *Meade-King, Robinson & Company Ltd* and it has offices in Liverpool, Leeds and Glasgow. *MKR* is now one of the largest independent suppliers of petrochemical-based products within the United Kingdom and employs about 30 people. The current chairman of the board, Mr Graeme de Bracy Marrs (Member of the Order of the

BERTRAM FLETCHER ROBINSON

British Empire), is a great-great-great-nephew of Joseph
Fletcher Robinson.

By 1868, Joseph was employing Richard Robinson as a
'general broker's apprentice'. During that same year, Rosa
Robinson died aged only 44 years. Her death was
registered in the district of West Derby, Lancashire.

On 2nd June 1869, 42 year-old Joseph married 28 year-old
Emily Hobson (BFR's mother) at the parish church of
Farndon in the district of Great Boughton, Chester,
Cheshire. Emily was born in Liverpool and was the
daughter of William Hobson (BFR's maternal grandfather),
a 'hosier, laceman and shop proprietor' of 86 Bold Street,
Liverpool. She was one of 7 children and her siblings
(BFR's maternal aunts and uncles) were called Alfred,
Mary, Fred, Fanny and Ann. The remaining child died
during infancy.

Joseph and Emily's marriage was witnessed by a 26 year-
old local merchant called Charles Holt. He belonged to an
influential family of 'chemists and druggists' and appears
to have married one of Emily's sisters. Charles and Emily
also attended services at the Renshaw Street Chapel with
Joseph. Following their marriage, Joseph and Emily set-up
home at 80 Rose Lane, Mossley Vale, Wavertree. It was
here that BFR was born on Monday 22nd August 1870.
This address is now the site of a commercial premises
belonging to Continuous Dataprint (UK) Limited (74-82
Rose Lane, Mossley Hill, Liverpool, Merseyside, L18
8EE). It is situated adjacent to Mossley Hill Railway
Station (see Plate 6).

Plate 6. The former site of 80 Rose Lane,
Mossley Vale, Wavertree, (BFR's birthplace).

On 1st January 1874, Joseph wrote to his customers
informing them that he had entered into partnership with a
23 year-old former 'produce apprentice' called Richard
Meade-King. Joseph continued to work as the 'commercial
manager' whilst Richard Meade-King acted as his
'financial partner'. Richard was the son of Joseph's
wealthy friend, Henry Meade-King, a retired merchant and
land-owner of 184 Sandfield Park, West Derby, Liverpool.
In that same letter, Joseph informed his clients of both a
change in business name and trading address as follows:

> On and after the 1st of January 1874, any
> business will be carried on under the name of
> Robinson and Meade-King of 7 Knowsley
> Buildings, Tithebarn Street, Liverpool, a more
> commodious and central office than 9 Orange
> Court.

8

During April 1881, Joseph and Emily were residing at 6, Lyndhurst Road, Wavertree. Meanwhile, BFR (10 years) was a boarder at a small independent school called Penkett Road Beach House at Liscard, New Brighton, West Cheshire. This school was located some 7 miles from BFR's family home and was owned by a retired farmer called Oswald Bayner. The school comprised of 4 teachers, 4 servants and 8 pupils including BFR. The teachers were 45 year-old Martha Bayner, 30 year-old Edith Robinson (no relation), 25 year-old Harrieta Brown and 20 year-old Ellen Dell. BFR's fellow students were Herbert Fayer (10 years), Theodore Grubb (8 years), Charles Knight (8 years), Samuel Park (11 years), Frances Puckering (9 years), Joseph Ruston (11 years) and Henry Wusdell (11 years).

During late 1881, Joseph retired and appointed his nephew, 27 year-old Richard Robinson, to replace him as commercial manager of the newly renamed *Meade-King, Robinson & Company*. This company had recently relocated to new premises situated at 11 Old Hall Street, Liverpool. By Easter 1882, Joseph, Emily and BFR had moved to Park Hill House, Park Hill Cross at Ipplepen in Devon.

Chapter 2

Devon

Park Hill House Estate was constructed around 1850 for a 'cider merchant' called John Bowden. It comprised of a large house, a neighbouring farm, multiple outbuildings and many acres of land (see Plate 7). During 1866, John Bowden funded the construction of Ipplepen Methodist Church and by 1878 he was trading as a 'corn factor, commission and general merchant' within both Plymouth and Wolborough-with-Newton Abbot. The original Park Hill Estate has since been annexed into a separate house and farm. Furthermore, Park Hill House has been redeveloped into 5 separate flats.

Plate 7. Park Hill House.

It is unclear why Joseph left Liverpool and moved to Ipplepen (during 1881, the population of each settlement was 611,075 and 816 respectively). Indeed, Liverpool was home to many of his family and friends and it is situated some 270 miles to the north of Ipplepen. One possible explanation is that Joseph had visited Devon whilst working as a 'commercial traveller' and decided to retire there in order to pursue his interest in equestrian-sports. He might even have visited Park Hill House itself in order to continue trading with John Bowden. Indeed, a 'cider merchant' of that same name is recorded as trading at 54 Berry Street, Liverpool, until 1849. Interestingly, on 3rd June 1902, a 'Bowden' acted as a witness to the marriage between BFR and Gladys Morris in London.

In any event, the Robinson family settled quickly into village life and they were well regarded for their charitable disposition. For example, Joseph contributed to the cost of general improvement work at St. Andrew's Church, Ipplepen. This work included renovating the windows and repositioning the organ (see Plate 8). During 1882, Joseph was appointed churchwarden and he befriended all three rectors during his period in that office: The Revd Robert Harris (1862-1887), The Revd Douglas Stewart (1887-1897) and The Revd Robert Duins Cooke (1897-1939). Interestingly, during 1901, the latter man accompanied BFR on a trip to Dartmoor to research the setting for *The Hound of the Baskervilles* (see Chapter 6).

Plate 8. St. Andrew's Church (circa 1900).

11

Plate 9. C. Seale-Hayne (circa 1885).

Joseph's interests quickly expanded beyond the spiritual welfare of the parishioners of Ipplepen. For example, he joined the committees of the Newton Abbot Board of Guardians, Local School Board and Newton Abbot Hospital. Joseph also joined the Devonshire Association (from 1884) and rode with both the South Devonshire Hunt and Dart Vale Harriers (until 1895). Furthermore, he joined Ipplepen Liberal Club and was befriended by the Liberal Member of Parliament for Mid-Devon, Sir Charles Seale-Hayne (see Plate 9).   Sir Charles represented this constituency between 1887 and 1903 and a character of both that same title and name is referred to in *The Hound of the Baskervilles*. Shortly before his death in 1903, Joseph was also appointed a justice-of-the peace for South Devon.

In April 1882, BFR was enrolled as a dayboy at a nearby independent school called Newton Abbot Proprietary

College in Wolborough (see Plate 10). This school was founded during 1861 by The Revd E. H. Cole. During 1869, 'Newton College' was registered as a limited liability company and The Right Honourable William Reginald, Earl of Devon, was appointed president of the Governing Council. By the early 1900's Newton College was marketing itself within the local press and other publications. For example, the following advertisement appeared in a book by A. J. Rhodes entitled *Newton Abbot: Its History and Development* that was published by the *Mid Devon Times* newspaper group (circa 1904):

> "**Preparation for the Army and Navy, the Universities, Professional & Commercial life**. LARGE PLAYING FIELDS. SWIMMING POOL AND EVERY REQUISITE OF A PUBLIC SCHOOL."

These additional requisites included: rugby pitches, cricket-field, pavilion (see Plate 11), gymnasium, racquet courts, fives courts, chapel, reading room, sitting rooms, laboratory, classrooms and library (to which, Joseph had made a sizeable donation upon BFR's admission to the school). These facilities were located in or about two sizable boarding houses called School-House and Red House (also referred to as Clayfield Lodge). Adjacent to the senior campus was a third and semi-autonomous boarding house called Newton Hall that catered for junior boys.

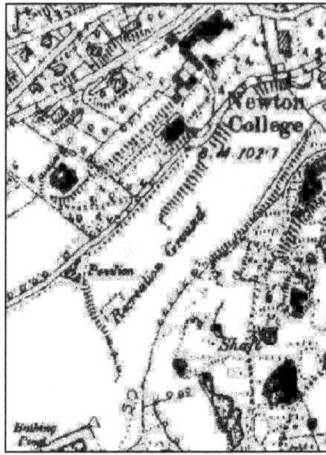

Plate 10. A map that features Newton College campus.

Plate 11. Newton College cricket pavilion (foreground) and
campus (rear and right).

Newton College enjoyed a regional reputation for scholastic
and sporting excellence. It reached a zenith during 1893
with 170 pupils but thereafter declined steadily: in 1924

there were 146 pupils and by 1937 just 47 pupils. The school was closed during 1939 and many of the remaining boys and staff were transferred to Newton House at Kelly College, Tavistock. The former Newton College campus was reopened as Forde Park Home Office Approved School (1940-1973). Devon County Council then used the site as a residential educational facility for vulnerable young people. In the 1990's, the site was sold to 'Barratt Developments PLC' and all existing buildings were demolished and replaced with modern homes (Hillside Estate).

The former Newton College sport field still exists and it is jointly used by Devon County Council, Devon County Football Association and Newton Abbot Athletic Football Club. The latter organisation now plays its home matches on the site of the old Newton College cricket-pitch and they also incorporated the pavilion into their new clubhouse facility. During the 1990's, the 'Newton College' bathing pond/swimming pool was filled-in and it was reopened as Decoy Bicycle Motocross Track (1998).

BFR's head master was The Revd George Townsend Warner (1841-1902). He had played first-class cricket for both Cambridge University and the Marylebone Cricket Club (1860-1863). Later, The Revd Warner represented the Gentleman of Devonshire Cricket Club (1870-1872) and captained Devon County Cricket Club (1883). He also became a member of the Rugby Football Union (1892-1896) and was the paternal grandfather of the noted English writer, Sylvia Townsend Warner (1893-1978).

Shortly before BFR's arrival, the future author, critic and academic, Arthur Quiller-Couch (see Plate 12), won a scholarship from Newton College to study at Clifton College. He wrote extensively under the pseudonym of 'Q'. Interestingly, Quiller-Couch met with BFR's future friend, Arthur Conan Doyle (hereafter ACD) on 6th March 1892. On 28th July 1884, he returned to Newton College and played cricket with The Revd Warner for an Old-Newtonians XI. Quiller-Couch later wrote in his autobiography entitled *Memories and Opinions* (Cambridge University Press, 1944) that The Revd Warner was:

> A tall sanguine man, in the middle years, but athletic yet, a rare runner between wickets; in school, and out of it, an organiser: a gentleman with every attribute of a good Head Master save a sense of justice, of which he had scarcely a glimmer, and being choleric, could be angriest when most unjust.

Plate 12. Sir Arthur Quiller-Couch (1863-1944).
COURTESY OF THE TOPFOTO COLLECTION.

Whilst at Newton College, BFR commenced a life-long friendship with a fellow-pupil called Harold Gaye

BERTRAM FLETCHER ROBINSON

Michelmore (1871-1957). Later, Michelmore (see Plate 13) became a solicitor and acted as the legal representative for the Robinson family. During 1949, he had a letter published in *The Western Morning News* that recalled BFR's literary collaborations with ACD (see Chapter 5).

Interestingly, both BFR and Michelmore were contemporaries of another notable Old-Newtonian called Percy Harrison Fawcett (1867-1925). Between 1906 and 1909, Fawcett (see Plate 14) undertook an expedition to map the borderland between Bolivia and Brazil. On 13th February 1911, he visited The Royal Geographical Society in London and delivered a lecture entitled *Further Exploration in Bolivia*. During this meeting, Fawcett mentioned a 1908 trip to the Ricardo Franco Falls in Brazil. It appears that ACD was also present at that meeting because Fawcett later wrote the following related comments in his posthumously published memoirs entitled *Exploration Fawcett* (London: Hutchinson, 1953, p. 122):

...monsters from the dawn of man's existence might still roam these heights unchallenged, imprisoned and protected by unscalable cliffs. So thought Conan Doyle when later in London I spoke of these hills and showed photographs of them. He mentioned an idea for a novel on Central South America and asked for information, which I told him I should be glad to supply. The fruit of it was his LOST WORLD in 1912, appearing as a serial in the STRAND MAGAZINE [sic], and subsequently in the form of a book that achieved widespread popularity.

Plate 13. Harold Michelmore (circa 1950).
COURTESY OF HAROLD MICHELMORE SOLICITORS.

BERTRAM FLETCHER ROBINSON

Plate 14. Percy Fawcett (circa 1920).
COURTESY OF THE TOPFOTO COLLECTION.

Like many private schools at that time, Newton College published a school magazine entitled *The Newtonian*. This was a monthly periodical that was distributed to parents and other prestigious educational institutions. *The Newtonian* published articles that were principally concerned with the school but it also featured essays on historical, theological and literary matters. Each year, the issues were collated into a leather-bound volume and republished by a local printer and stationer called G.H. Hearder of Wolborough Street, Newton Abbot.

During the Summer Term of 1883, *The Newtonian* featured an anonymous essay entitled *Recent Artic Explorations* (Vol. 8, Issue No. 66, pp 65-68). It was written following a visit to the school by one W. Grant. During the spring of 1882, he served aboard a ship called the *Kara* and

19

participated in the rescue of the crew from a ship called the *Eira*. The *Eira* sank near the coast of Franz-Josef Land in late 1881 and those aboard narrowly survived the ensuing winter by constructing ice-huts. The *Kara* was assisted in this rescue by a steam-whaler called the *Hope*. This story is interesting in so far that ACD worked as an unqualified surgeon aboard the *Hope* in 1880. During that voyage, ACD fell from the ice into a freezing sea and narrowly avoided drowning by using a skinned seal carcass to pull himself out.

During the Spring Term of 1884, *The Newtonian* featured a 3000-word essay entitled *American Literature and Humour* (Vol. 9, Issue No. 73, pp 46-50). This article discusses the relative merits of American authors including Henry James, William Dean Howells, Artemus Ward, Mark Twain and Bret Harte. It is by-lined 'B' and appears to be the first published article written by BFR. Certainly, BFR later wrote about American literature for the *Daily Express* newspaper (1900-1904) and he was variously nicknamed 'Bobbles', 'Bertie' and 'Bobby'. Interestingly, the article also refers to a book by Oliver Wendell Holmes entitled *Autocrat at the Breakfast Table*. During 1984, the Sherlockian, Michael Harrison, wrote a book entitled *A Study in Surmise* in which, he conjectured that ACD used the surnames of both Oliver Wendell Holmes and a real-life detective called Wendel Scherer, to derive the name 'Sherlock Holmes'.

During the Christmas Term of 1888, *The Newtonian* featured an article entitled *The Annual Prize Day* (Vol. 13, Issue No. 113, pp 129-135). It records that The Revd Warner had recently presented a report about the 'Lower

BERTRAM FLETCHER ROBINSON

Certificate' for the 'Oxford and Cambridge Schools Examination Board' to an assembly of parents, boys and local dignitaries. It was dated 30th August 1888 and addressed *"To the Chairman of the Governing Body of Newton College"*. Extracts from this report together with relevant examination results are listed in full below:

[The letters prefixed to the candidate's names indicate the subjects in which they passed].

a = Latin
i = Scripture
b = Greek
j = English
c = French
k = English History
d = German
l = Geography
f = Arithmetic
m = Chemistry
g = Additional Mathematics
o = Geometrical Drawing

[A capital letter denotes that a First Class was obtained in the subject indicated by the letter.]

NAME OF PUPIL:	SUBJECTS:
Michelmore, Harold Gaye	*a, b, F, g, i.*
Robinson, Bertram Fletcher	*a, b, g, I, J, K, l.*

21

"Arithmetic. There were 25 candidates from this School. Several excellent papers were sent up, two obtaining full marks...Highly commended...H. G. Michelmore..."

"English History - General. ...Robinson deserves special mention for an admirable paper; the rest seem to show that hardly sufficient attention is paid to the subject."

During the Christmas Term of 1889, *The Newtonian* reported that BFR had played rugby as a forward for a 'Past and Present Newton College XV' against Devonshire. The match was played in front 'of a good number of spectators' at the ground of Newton Town (Newton Abbot). Devonshire won the game by a score of 4 goals to 2 tries (12 points to 2 points). Two members of the 'Newton College XV' were subsequently selected to represent the county team. The full team list for each side was as follows:

Newtonians. C.W.C. Ingles (Jesus College, Cambridge), (back); C.W. Hayward (Newton College), F.W. Marshall (Teignmouth), C.V. Windsor (Newton College), A.A. Bearne (Edinburgh University), (¾ backs); G.F. Davies (Newton College), E.L.L. Hammond (Newton College), (½ backs); E.N. Gardiner (Newton College), (Capt.), R.D. Williams (Emmanuel College, Cambridge), L.R. Biddell (Exeter), H. Osmond (Exeter), R.A. O'Neill (Newton College), B.F. Robinson (Newton College), J.C. Alsop (Newton College), W. St. A. Wake (Newton College), (forwards).

Devon County. Hayman (Exeter), (back); A.M. Sutthery (Exeter), (Capt.), M.H. Toller (Barnstaple), F.H. Davies

BERTRAM FLETCHER ROBINSON

([Plymouth] Albion), (¾ backs); F.W. Herring (Tiverton), J. Davies (Torquay Athletic), (½ backs); W. Ashford (Exeter), M.W. Ball (Newton), B. Bennett (Torquay Athletic), A.G. Frith (Tiverton), C. Hawking (Torquay Athletic), Rev. T.W. Hudson (Newton), F.H. Toller (Barnstaple), S.R. Wallis (Exeter), W.S.S. Wilson (Dartmouth), (forwards).

The master responsible for rugby at Newton College during BFR's final years was Edward Norman Gardiner. Gardiner played at least six rugby matches as a forward for Devonshire (1887-1890) and the English Western Counties (1888/89). He evidently had a good relationship with BFR because they served together on various school committees that included the debating society, athletic sports and rugby football. In September 1888, Gardiner supported BFR's election to the prestigious position of 'Second Captain of School House'. During 1896, BFR wrote a book entitled *Rugby Football* (London: A.D. Innes & Company) in which, he states that Gardiner provided him with 'excellent advice in football matters' (see Chapter 4). Later, Gardiner achieved distinction as a leading scholar on the topic of classical sports. He wrote various books including *Athletic Sports and Festivals* (1910) and *Athletics in the Ancient World* (1930).

The Newtonian includes many other references to BFR that span the period of his schooling at Newton College (April 1882 - April 1890). Collectively, these entries portray a gregarious, sporting and responsible individual with a passion for literature, theology and history. The most notable of these additional entries are listed overleaf:

23

BERTRAM FLETCHER ROBINSON

Winner of a 'Special Prize for English' (16th December 1882); Winner of the 'Junior Prize for Divinity' (31st July 1883); Winner of the 'Archdeacon Earle's Prize for Divinity' (1888); Winner of the 'Senior Prize for History' (1888); 1st XV Rugby Team (1888-1890); 1st XI Cricket Team (1888-1890); Winner of the High Jump Prize at the School Annual Sports (21st April 1888); 2nd Captain School-House (1888/1889); Secretary of the School Debating Society (1888-1890); Member of the School Library Committee (1888/1889), Editor of *The Newtonian* (1887-1889).

Chapter 3

Cambridge University

During April 1890, 19 year-old BFR departed Newton College and was admitted to Cambridge University. It is interesting to note that during that same year, an Ipplepen-born journalist called Alfred Langler (1865-1928), also departed Devon and emigrated to South Australia (see Plate 15). Like BFR, he too became a newspaper editor and was a practising Christian. It appears likely that both men had attended the same services at St. Andrew's Church and were well acquainted. During 1926, Langler became chairman of the board of directors of the new West Australian Newspapers Ltd. and he was knighted the following year. It is a striking coincidence that two successful future journalists were residents of the same small village at the same time.

Plate 15. Alfred Langler.
STATE LIBRARY OF SOUTH AUSTRALIA. ALL RIGHTS RESERVED (B16256)

BERTRAM FLETCHER ROBINSON

BFR read History at Jesus College (see Plate 16) and was elected an 'Exhibitioner' (meaning that his tuition fees were subsidised by his college). 'Jesus' was founded in 1496 by the Bishop of Ely on the site of a Benedictine convent. It is traditionally maintained that the convent was turned into a college because it had gained a reputation for licentiousness. The college's full name is *The College of the Blessed Virgin Mary, Saint John the Evangelist and the glorious Virgin Saint Radegund, near Cambridge.* Its common name derives from the name of its chapel that was constructed at the beginning of the 11th century and is the oldest building still in use at Cambridge University.

Plate 16. Jesus College (1842).
COURTESY OF DR. FRANCIS WILLMOTH.

26

Plate 17. F.D. Browne (sat 2nd row & centre).
COURTESY OF ISLA BROWNLESS.

During October 1885, the Jesus College chaplain and lecturer, Frederick John Foakes-Jackson, founded a periodical entitled *The Chanticleer* (renamed *The Chanticlere* from October 1892).   It was edited by a committee comprising of Foakes-Jackson and several undergraduates and was published by a local printer called J. Palmer of Jesus Lane. At the beginning of each term, *The Chanticleer* and *The Chanticlere* would print a review of events that had taken place at Jesus College during the previous term.   Hence, these records provide a near contemporaneous account of BFR's life as a student in Cambridge.

During the early 1890's, Jesus College numbered only about 150 students. It enjoyed an excellent reputation for sport and the 'Varsity soccer, rugby and cricket teams were each captained by a 'Jesuan'. Indeed, no fewer than 18 Jesuans had recently been awarded 'Blues' (a sporting honour conferred upon a student who had competed at a sport against Oxford University).

The master of Jesus College between 1885 and 1912 was The Revd Dr. Henry Arthur Morgan (1830-1912). He was nicknamed 'Black Morgan' to distinguish him from the unrelated senior tutor and dean of Jesus College, The Revd Edmund Henry Morgan ('Red Morgan'). In 1862, Henry Morgan together with Leslie Stephen became the first mountaineers to ascend the 3,471-meter summit of Jungfraujoch in the Swiss Alps. The Revd Henry Morgan wrote extensively about academia, theology and geography. He was also pivotal in raising the profile of smaller colleges at Cambridge University.

Interestingly, The Revd Warner's son and namesake George Townsend Warner (1865-1916) was elected a 'Fellow' of Jesus College in 1890. George Warner studied at Jesus between 1884 and 1887 and won a Golf Blue. During 1887, he was awarded a first-class Tripos degree in History and he subsequently gained various prestigious scholarships. This might explain why 11 Old-Newtonians including BFR elected to enter Jesus College between 1886 and 1894 (a further 8 entered other colleges at Cambridge during that same period). During spring 1890, George Warner was also elected president of the Jesus College Debating Society that was commonly referred to as the 'Cranmer'. He later acted as History examiner in the same year that BFR was awarded a History degree. George Warner's daughter was the distinguished English writer, Sylvia Townsend Warner (1893-1978).

BERTRAM FLETCHER ROBINSON

During the May Term of 1890, BFR was reacquainted with an old school friend called Francis Deshon Browne (see Plate 17). He was the son of James Francis Browne, the Archdeacon of Madras. Francis Browne was secretary of the Jesus College 1st boat (1890-1891) and had rowed for the 1st VIII in an inter-collegiate competition called the 'May Bumps'. He was also a member of the Jesus Drama Society called the 'Halliwell' and later played for the college rugby 1st XV and cricket 2nd XI. Later, Browne was ordained as a deacon (1895) and a priest (1897), before eventually becoming the head master of Lambrook School in Berkshire (1904-1930). He is perhaps best remembered for commissioning the construction of a beautiful chapel at this school during his first year there. Undoubtedly, Browne helped BFR settle in to college life and also influenced his choice of extra-curricular activities. Indeed, the English Census records that both men visited Park Hill House together during April 1891. BFR frequently returned to Ipplepen during his holidays (see Plate 18).

Plate 18. The 1891 Ipplepen Cricket XI featuring BFR (stood 3rd from left) and Henry 'Harry' Baskerville (sat 2nd from right) [see Chapter 6].

BERTRAM FLETCHER ROBINSON

During October 1890, BFR was befriended by a 21 year-old Jesuan called Percy Holden Illingworth. He was the grandson of Sir Isaac Holden and the brother of Albert Holden Illingworth (later 1st Baron Illingworth). Illingworth entered Jesus College during October 1887 and he was a former captain of the university rugby team (1889/90) and a double Rugby Blue (1889 & 1890). He also played in the 1891 annual Northern England v. Southern England rugby match at Richmond in Surrey. Furthermore, Illingworth was captain of the Jesus 1st VIII boat (1890-1891) and later, he narrowly missed gaining a Rowing Blue when he was selected as 9th man for the annual Oxford and Cambridge Boat Race of 1893 (see Plate 19). After completing his studies (1892), Illingworth became a barrister-at-law, served in the 2nd Boer War and was elected as a Liberal MP for Shipley in Yorkshire (1906-1915). Illingworth then held various junior government posts before being appointed chief whip (1912-1915).

Plate 19. The 1893 Cambridge 1st VIII featuring
Trevor Lewis and Percy Illingworth (ninth-man).
COURTESY OF THE PATRICK CASEY COLLECTION.

Plate 20. Arthur Hammond Marshall.
COURTESY OF THE TOPFOTO COLLECTION.

BERTRAM FLETCHER ROBINSON

During October 1890, BFR and Illingworth met two Trinity College 'freshmen' (a term used to describe a newly enrolled undergraduate) and all four men became friends. Twenty year-old Trevor Gwyn Elliot Lewis of Aberdare, Glamorgan, Wales, was the son of Sir William Lewis (later 1st Baron Merthyr) and the younger brother of Hubert Clerk Lewis (later 2nd Baron Merthyr). Trevor Lewis (see Plate 19) later became a barrister-at-law (19th November 1894) and disclaimed his father's title during 1911. Twenty-four year-old Arthur Hammond Marshall (see Plate 20) was from Raven Hall, Scarborough, Yorkshire and became an author and writer for *Punch* (under the pseudonym 'Archibald Marshall'). During 1933, Marshall had an autobiography published that is entitled *Out and About: Random Reminiscences* (London: John Murray). In Chapter 1, Marshall recalls his undergraduate days and gives a detailed account about the relationships between himself, BFR, Illingworth and Lewis.

During October 1890, BFR played his first match for Jesus College Rugby Football Club. On 5th November 1891, he made his debut appearance as a forward for Cambridge University Rugby Football Club in a match that was played against Lancashire. Between October 1890 and March 1894, BFR played approximately 80 games for both Jesus and Cambridge (including tour games). He clearly believed that rugby demanded self-discipline because he later wrote the following comment in his book entitled *Rugby Football* (1896):

> Perhaps the best feature of this enthusiasm
> for Rugby Football which has grown up

---

amongst working men is the delight in hard exercise and consequent self-denial that it has taught him. A man cannot spend his nights and his wages in the public-house if twice a week he has to face a hard struggle of forty minutes each way.

BFR participated in 5 particularly notable first-class rugby matches during his time as a student at Cambridge. He twice played for a combined 'Varsity XV' (Oxford & Cambridge) against a combined London, Southern, Western and Midland Counties XV (1892 & 1893). This annual fixture was one of several games that international selectors used to pick teams for England, Ireland, Scotland and Wales. BFR's obituary in the *Daily Express* reports that he would have played for England but for an 'accident'. He also played 3 games against Oxford University thereby gaining the rare distinction of becoming a triple Rugby Blue (see Plates 21-23). The last of these 3 matches was the 21st annual 'Varsity match and it was played on 13th December 1893 at the Queen's Club in London. Oxford won the game by a score of 1 try to nil (3 points to 0 points). A match report in *The Times* newspaper reveals that 'many thousand' watched this game and that the 2 teams had fielded 15 international players as follows:

Cambridge University: (Back); E* E. Field (Clifton & Trinity). (¾ backs); S* J.J. Gowans (Harrow & Clare), S+** W. Neilson (Merchiston & Clare), W.G. Druce (Marlborough & Trinity), L.E. Pilkington (Clifton & King's). (½ backs); A.H. Greg (Marlborough & Trinity), E R.O. Schwarz (St. Paul's & Christ's). (Forwards); W*** C.B. Nicholl (Llandovery College & Queen's), E* W.E. Tucker (Trinity College, Port Hope, Canada & Caius), ** B.F. Robinson (Newton Abbot & Jesus), E A.F. Todd (Mill Hill & Caius), * H.D. Rendall (Rugby & Trinity), E F. Mitchell (St. Peter's School, York & Trinity), S.E.A. Whiteway (Sedbergh & Trinity), H. Laing (Wellington & Trinity).

BERTRAM FLETCHER ROBINSON

Oxford University: (Back); * L.C. Humfrey (Christ's College, Brecon & Keble). (¾ backs); S H.T.S. Gedge (Loretto & Keble), W+** J. Conway-Rees (Llandovery College & Jesus), E E.M. Baker (Denstone & Keble), W W.Ll. Thomas (Christ College, Brecon & Keble). (½ backs); S* W.P. Donaldson (Loretto & Brasenose), E R.H.B. Cattell (Trinity College, Stratford-on-Avon & Exeter). (Forwards); * C.D. Baker Sherborne & Merton), * A.H. Colville (Merchant Taylors' in Crosby & Merton), E** F.O. Poole (Cheltenham & Keble), R.B. Littlewood (Merchant Taylors' in London & Wadham), * J. A. Smith (Loretto & Trinity), D.W. Donaldson (Loretto & New College), * A.C: Elwes (Bedford Grammar School & St. John's), E.R. Balfour (Edinburgh Academy and University).

(Key: *E* = England, *I* = Ireland, *S* = Scotland, *W* = Wales, * = Blue, + = Captain).

Plate 21. The 1891/92 Cambridge University
1st XV Rugby Team
featuring BFR (sat 1st right in middle row).
COURTESY OF THE PATRICK CASEY COLLECTION.

34

BERTRAM FLETCHER ROBINSON

Plate 22. The 1892/93 Cambridge University 1st XV Rugby Team featuring BFR (sat 1st right in middle row).

Plate 23. The 1893/94 Cambridge University 1st XV Rugby Team featuring BFR (sat 2nd right in middle row).
COURTESY OF THE PATRICK CASEY COLLECTION.

BERTRAM FLETCHER ROBINSON

During June 1892, BFR was selected to row as 5th oar for the Jesus 1st VIII in the first division of the May Bumps (then a biannual intercollegiate race held over a four-day period). Traditionally, this position was filled by someone who possessed weight, power and stamina. At that time, BFR stood 6 foot and 3 inches tall and weighed 13 stone and 5 pounds (or 1.9 meters and 84.8 kilograms respectively). On the final day, Illingworth cut his hand so 'severely' that he was unable to row for the remainder of that season. Throughout the races, the Jesus 1st boat was widely agreed to be 'one of the fastest on the river'. Nevertheless, they ended the races in 7th position within a field that comprised of 15 boats. The full names and weights of the Jesus 1st VIII was as follows:

BERTRAM FLETCHER ROBINSON

Position:	Name:	Stones:	Pounds:
Bow	*B Middleditch	9	12
2	D R Dangar	11	5
3	#C E Fitch	11	1
4	~F E Allhusen	12	1
5	OB F Robinson	13	5
6	A Bogle	11	7
7	xR G Neill	12	3
Stroke	+P H Illingworth	11	0
Cox	A H Baker	8	8

*Played soccer Cambridge University ('Blue' 1895) England (1897).
#Played rugby for Cambridge University ('Blue' 1889).
~Donor of the 'Allhusen Cup' to Jesus College Boat Club.
oPlayed rugby for Cambridge University ('Blue' 1891, 1892 & 1893).
xRowed for Cambridge University ('Blue' 1892).
+Played rugby for Cambridge University ('Blue' 1889 & 1890).

On 4th July 1892, BFR and seven other 'Jesuans' procured rooms from one Mrs. Wiggins at Saragossa House in New Street, Henley-on-Thames, Oxfordshire. They went there to represent Jesus College Boat Club in the Thames Challenge Cup at the Henley Royal Regatta. The crew were accompanied by Illingworth and their coach, Thomas Edward Hockin (1854-1923). Illingworth was the first

BERTRAM FLETCHER ROBINSON

choice stroke for Jesus College but was unable to row due to the recent injury to his hand. Hockin was a quadruple Rowing Blue, having represented Cambridge University in four 'Varsity Boat Races during his time as a Jesus College undergraduate (1876, 1877, 1878 & 1879). The full team was as follows:

Position:	Name:	Stones:	Pounds:
Bow	*B Middleditch	9	11
2	D R Dangar	11	9
3	A H Busby	10	7
4	#F E Allhusen	12	1
5	xB F Robinson	13	5
6	A Bogle	11	7
7	+C E Fitch	11	11
Stroke	~R G Neill	11	12
Cox	A H Baker	8	13

*Played soccer Cambridge University ('Blue' 1895), England (1897).
#Donor of the 'Allhusen Cup' to the Jesus College Boat Club.
xPlayed rugby for Cambridge University ('Blue' 1891, 1892 & 1893).
~Rowed for Cambridge University ('Blue' 1892).
+Played rugby for Cambridge University ('Blue' 1889).

BERTRAM FLETCHER ROBINSON

On 7th July 1892, Jesus College Boat Club and Trinity College Boat Club contested the final heat for the Thames Challenge Cup. A reasonable crowd was in attendance and the weather was described as being 'beautifully fine' but blustery. The race was contested over a distance of 1.31 miles (2112 meters) and Jesus won in a time of 8 minutes and 10 seconds. *The Times* newspaper reported this race as follows (8th July, p. 4):

> Jesus came away at the start, and were a third of a length in advance at the top of the island, and increased their lead to three parts at the quarter-mile post, and nearly two lengths at Fawley Court Boathouse. Continuing to gain steadily, Jesus led by upwards of two lengths at the mile mark, and keeping in front to the finish won by four lengths...

The news of this victory was warmly received by the Jesuan fraternity and it generated optimism for the future prospects of college rowing. This reaction is encapsulated by the following comment that was published in *The Chanticlere* (Issue No. 22, p.16):

> It is now eight years since the Jesus Boat was head of the river [1886] and three years ago [1889] the Boat Club was in so bad a way that it seemed well nigh hopeless to think of reaching such a height again...Then came a change, the new Captain [Illingworth] was keen and the freshmen willing, with the result that at

Henley four of that year were rowing in the boat. We know too that the present Captain [R. G. Neill] is by no means lacking in keenness, and that it will not be his fault if the boat does not go up again this year. Dare we hope to be second on the river...

This reaction to the victory evidently made a deep impression upon BFR. During February 1894, he was selected for the Cambridge University 'Trial Eight' and narrowly missed gaining a rowing 'Blue'. After departing Cambridge, BFR became involved with two books about rowing (see Chapter 4) and also wrote a series of articles about the 'Varsity Boat Race for the *Daily Express* newspaper. Furthermore, on 4th July 1906, he published one of his own short stories in *Vanity Fair* that is entitled *In Which a Hero of Henley Suffers Adversity* (pp. 18-19).

Plate 24. Rudolph Chambers Lehmann.
COURTESY OF THE TOPFOTO COLLECTION.

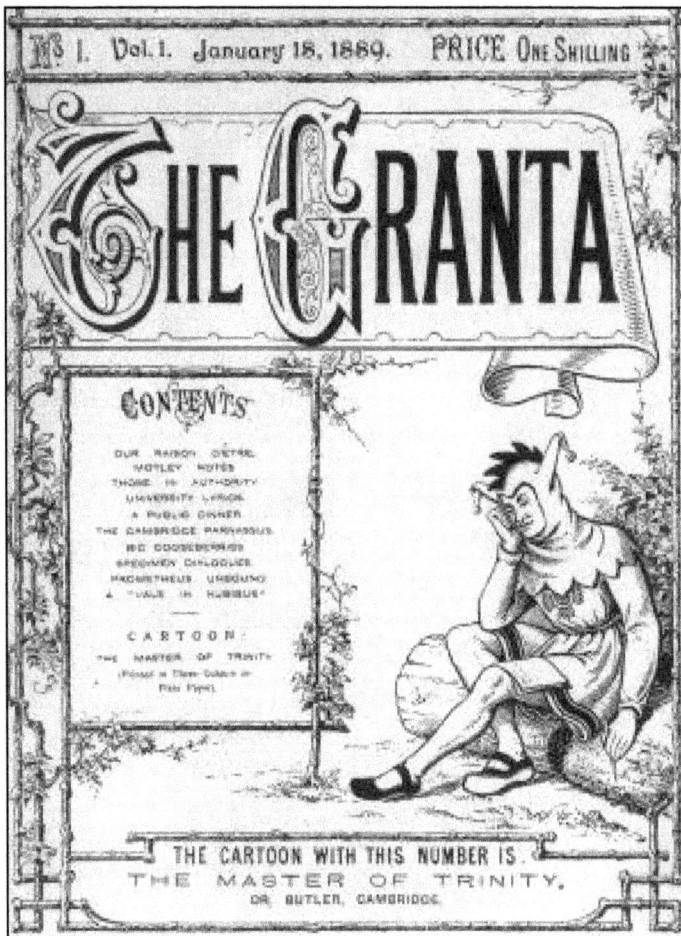

Plate 25. *The Granta* (1889).

During October 1892, BFR was employed by Rudolph Chambers Lehmann (see Plate 24) to work as the rugby contributor for *The Granta* (published by W. P. Spalding, Cambridge). Lehmann had co-founded *The Granta* four years earlier and was both proprietor and editor (see Plate

25). Lehmann was a former student at Trinity College (1874-1878), president of the Cambridge University Society (1876-1877) and a qualified barrister-at-law (21st April 1880). *The Granta* first appeared on 18th January 1889 (published by King, Sell & Railton Ltd, Fleet Street, London) shortly after Lehmann was defeated as the Liberal Party Parliamentary candidate for East Hull. It catered for the rising demand amongst students for 'light-verse of topical interest'. Later, Lehmann replaced BFR's uncle, John Robinson, as editor of the London *Daily News* (1901-1902) and was elected as a Liberal MP for the Harborough Division of Leicestershire (1906-1910).

Lehmann lived in London where he was both an active member of the Liberal Reform Club and wrote for *Punch* (1889-1919). Thereafter he was appointed as the coach of the Cambridge 'Varsity rowing team (1893), honorary secretary to the British Amateur Rowing Association (1893-1901) and captain of the Leander Rowing Club (1894-1896). In order to accommodate these other interests, Lehmann appointed a series of student sub-editors (or 'Cambridge editors') to manage *The Granta*. One such sub-editor, Charles Geake, recalled this arrangement in a letter that he sent to *The Granta* on 30th November 1901:

> Lehmann came-up [dined at his former college] every Thursday with almost unfailing regularity and on Thursday night we met to approve of the next Saturday's paper, and to plot out that of the Saturday after.

The Granta was primarily written for Cambridge undergraduates but it also reported on events at both Trinity

College (Dublin) and Oxford University. It was sold at each of these three institutions and also by independent retailers in London. The four sub-editors appointed by Lehmann were; Ernest Alfred Newton of King's (October 1889 - May 1890); Charles Geake of Clare (October 1890 - May 1892); Robert Pentland Mahaffy of King's (October 1892 - May 1893) and BFR of Jesus (October 1893 - April 1895). Mahaffy became a barrister-at-law and also wrote for the *Dublin Daily Express* (1899-1902). He later described his appointment as sub-editor of *The Granta* in a letter that was published in the same periodical:

> When I became Cambridge Editor in the autumn of 1892, there had been great changes in our staff at Cambridge. All our principal writers had gone down [graduated], especially the poets. I was left almost entirely without poets, rowing correspondents, football correspondents, or anything else. It is wonderful however, how quickly one finds poets; in a very few weeks I had discovered a new nest of singing bird ... B. F. Robinson, of Jesus, was my Rugby man, and afterwards, when he was editor of Vanity Fair and then of The World, I would tell him that I had launched him...

In addition to acting as the 'Rugby man' BFR had 15 poems, 1 lyrical verse and 1 playlet published in *The Granta* between 18th February 1893 and 23rd January 1897 (see Chapter 12). Hence, it was both Lehmann and Mahaffy who nurtured BFR's interest in journalism and writing. Indeed, BFR told Marshall that his uncle, John

Robinson, the then manager and editor of the London *Daily News*, had played no part in his eventual choice of profession.

On 16th December 1892, Lehmann and Mahaffy hosted the 3rd annual dinner for *The Granta* at the Reform Club, Pall Mall, London (see Plate 26). The dinner was also used to celebrate the pending publication of the 100th edition. Amongst the 20 guests who attended (see Plate 27), were ACD (the grandson of John 'HB' Doyle, a former *Punch* illustrator) and BFR's uncle, John Robinson. Both men were friends of a fellow Reformer called Thomas Wemyss Reid, the editor of the *Leeds Mercury* that is mentioned by Sherlock Holmes in *The Hound of the Baskervilles* (see Plate 28). The remaining guests were largely drawn from the staff of *The Granta* and *Punch*, which overlapped to such a degree that the former was called 'Punch with a little Cam water' and the latter 'the London Granta'.

Plate 26. Reform Club, Pall Mall, London

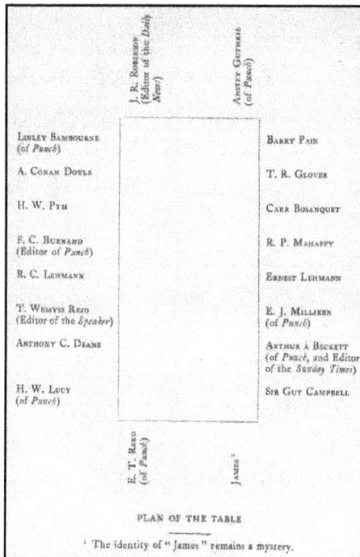

Plate 27. *Granta* seat-plan (1893).

BERTRAM FLETCHER ROBINSON

Shortly after this dinner was held, Lehmann began writing a series of early Sherlockian parodies entitled *The Adventures of Picklock Holes* (and Potson). The first 7 of these were published in *Punch* between 12th August 1893 and 23rd December 1893. Later, Lehmann wrote a further 8 items collectively entitled *The Return of Picklock Holes* that were first published in *Punch* between 1903 and 1904. It is not known whether ACD objected to these parodies but it is interesting to note that he did not attend any subsequent annual dinners hosted by staff from *The Granta*.

During June 1893, BFR sat Part I and II of the History Tripos examination. As previously mentioned, the then 'History Examiner' at Jesus College was the Old Newtonian, George Warner, son of BFR's former headmaster. The practice of assessing candidates known to an assessor is no longer regarded as safe educational practice. BFR was subsequently awarded a second-class Bachelor of Arts degree. Thereafter, he re-enrolled at Jesus College to study Law and successfully completed Part I of the Law Tripos during June 1894.

During October 1893, Lehmann appointed BFR to the position of sub-editor of *The Granta*. The most notable events during BFR's 18 month editorship were the retirement of a contributor called Barry Eric Odell Pain and the appointment of a contributor called Owen Seaman. At that time, Pain also wrote for *Punch*, *Speaker* and various London-based newspapers. Seaman had previously worked as a professor of literature at Durham University (1888-1893). Later, he also joined the staff of *Punch* (1897) and eventually became its editor (1906-1932). BFR wrote in

Vanity Fair that Seaman (see Plate 29) was one of the few who 'kept the light of parody burning amongst us.' (1st September 1904, p. 272). Seaman was knighted and appointed a Baronet during 1914 and 1933 respectively.

Plate 28. Thomas Wemyss Reid
COURTESY OF THE TOPFOTO COLLECTION

BERTRAM FLETCHER ROBINSON

Plate 29. Owen Seaman.
COURTESY OF THE TOPFOTO COLLECTION.

On 12th December 1893, Lehmann and BFR jointly hosted the 4th annual Granta dinner at the Reform Club. Notable guests included Arthur Hammond Marshall, Owen Seaman, Barry Pain and Thomas Wemyss Reid. Two days later, BFR and other members of the Cambridge University Rugby Football Club embarked upon a tour of the north of England and Scotland. On 17th December 1893, the tourists visited the Forth Bridge and were mistaken for 'the Monson case jury and some excitement was caused thereby.' Alfred John Monson was on trial at Edinburgh High Court for the suspected murder of a young nobleman called Cecil Hambrough. Despite much incriminating evidence, the case against Monson was eventually found 'not proven'. It is interesting to note that the prosecution witnesses included Dr. Joseph Bell, the Edinburgh surgeon, who had taught ACD and was the model for Sherlock Holmes.

BERTRAM FLETCHER ROBINSON

The Chanticleer and *The Chanticlere* include many other references to BFR that span the period of his studies at Jesus College (April 1890 – June 1894). Collectively, these entries portray an intelligent, popular and responsible individual with a passion for the arts, sport and student affairs. The most notable of these additional entries are listed below:

Elected as a member of both the Cranmer and Jesus College Common Room Debating Society (May Term 1890 and 19th February 1891 respectively); presented a paper entitled *Village Life in the 14th and 15th Centuries* to Jesus College Coleridge Society (Michaelmas Term 1890); elected honorary secretary of the Jesus College Common Room Debating Society (Lent and May Terms 1891); elected a member of the Halliwell Dramatic Society (Michaelmas Term 1891); elected as a committee member of the Cambridge University Rugby Union Football Club (12th Oct. 1892); participated in a rugby tour with Cambridge 1st XV to Ireland (Dec. 1892); elected as a committee member of the Jesus College Common Room (7th June 1893 & 24th January 1894); represented Jesus College Cricket XI (Summer holidays 1893); participated in a rugby-tour of Somerset and Devon with the Jesus College Wanderers XV (26th December 1893 – 4th January 1894).

Chapter 4

Post-Cambridge

Trevor Lewis graduated during the summer of 1894 and shortly thereafter, he rented a flat at 126 Ashley Gardens, Kensington, London (see Plate 30). Arthur Hammond Marshall reports in his autobiography that both Percy Illingworth and BFR resided with Lewis at that address for the next seven years. Indeed, *The Post Office London Directory* and the *London Electoral Roll* indicate that Lewis resided at 126 Ashley Gardens until 1907 and that Illingworth was a tenant between 1896 and 1902. However, BFR is not featured in either record. This raises the question as to where he lived between 1894 and 1901?

Between 1894 and 1896, BFR is listed in the Jesus College student-register. It therefore appears that he stayed in Cambridge and studied part-time for the Bar Examination whilst working as sub-editor of *The Granta* (1893-1895). Throughout that period and beyond, BFR paid regular visits to the Reform Club in London. During these visits it appears that he stayed with both Lewis and Illingworth. However, in 1901, BFR sent a dispatch from Cape Town to the offices of the *Daily Express* in which, he reports an encounter with a man from Newton Abbot and adds 'near which town I also live' (see Chapter 5). This implies that BFR resided at Jesus College and Ashley Gardens between 1894 and 1896, and Ashley Gardens and Park Hill House between 1896 and 1901.

BERTRAM FLETCHER ROBINSON

Plate 30. 126 Ashley Gardens,
Kensington, London (centre).

On 3rd November 1894, ACD wrote to BFR's uncle, Sir
John Robinson from Amherst House, Amherst,
Massachusetts, in the United Stated of America. At that
time, John Robinson was on the managing committee of the
Reform Club and ACD was also a member. In his letter,
ACD described the first five weeks of his first North
America lecture-tour and details the arrangements for his
return to England. ACD began this letter as follows:

MY DEAR ROBINSON

May I make you my mouth-piece in conveying
my warm remembrances to friends of the
Reform, above all to Payn and Reid?

ACD seldom addressed his friends by their Christian
names. It is interesting to note, that this same formal

BERTRAM FLETCHER ROBINSON

greeting was later used in two letters that acknowledge
BFR's assistance with the plot of *The Hound of the
Baskervilles* (see Chapter 6). Furthermore, as previously
stated, Thomas Wemyss Reid was editor of the *Leeds
Mercury*, a newspaper that is referred to by Sherlock
Holmes in that same story.

In April 1895, Lehmann sold *The Granta* to a Cambridge
graduate called St. John Basil Wynne Willson (later, the
Bishop of Bath & Wells). About that same time, BFR
resigned his position with *The Granta* and focused upon his
legal studies. During April 1896, he successfully sat the
Bar Examinations in London. On 17th June of that same
year, BFR accepted an invitation to the Inner Temple
thereby qualifying as a barrister-at-law. He subsequently
removed his name from the Jesus College student-register.
However, he never practised law and even delegated
personal legal matters to his Devon-based friend and
solicitor, Harold Gaye Michelmore (see Chapter 2). Harold
Michelmore & Company Solicitors still operate a practice
in Newton Abbot.

During 1896, BFR was commissioned to write a book
entitled *Rugby Football* for *The Isthmian Library* (see Plate
31). This book was edited by Max Pemberton (see Plate
32) and was published during October of that same year
(London: A. D. Innes and Company). It consists of 338
pages and 17 chapters and is illustrated throughout. It is
interesting to note that the final chapter was contributed by
the English rugby international, Henry Barrington Tristram,
a former master and rugby coach at Newton College
between 1883 and 1887 (see Plate 33).

52

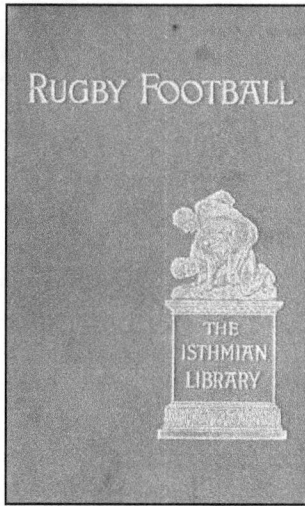

Plate 31. *Rugby Football* (1896).

Plate 32. Max Pemberton.

Plate 33. Henry Barrington Tristram.

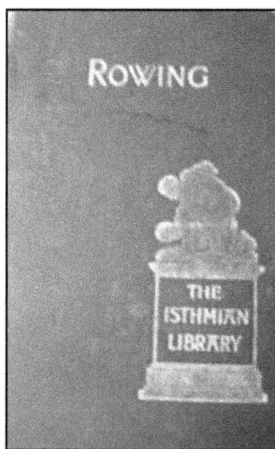

Plate 34. *Rowing* (1897).

Rugby Football was advertised in *The Times* newspaper on 14th October 1896 (p. 10), 30th October 1896 (p. 12), 14th December 1897 (p. 14), 17th December 1897 (p. 16) and 21st December 1897 (p. 12). The 2nd in this series of advertisements is particularly interesting because it is accompanied by various endorsements as follows:

"THE ISTHMIAN LIBRARY

has made more than a promising start." - Daily News.
"If succeeding issues of the new Isthmian Library Series keep up
the form of the initial volume its success is certain." - Referee.
"If the following volumes of the series are equal to the present,
they will, indeed, form a most useful library of sport." Birmingham Daily Post.

VOL. I. RUGBY FOOTBALL. By B.

FLETCHER ROBINSON. With Chapters by FRANK
MITCHELL, R. H. CATTELL, C. J. N.FLEMING, GREGOR
MACGREGOR, and H. B. TRISTRAM, and dedicated, by permis-
sion, to Mr. Rowland Hill.
Post 8vo., Cloth, 5s.

"His volume is nothing if not practical, yet it is eminently read-
able." - Daily News.
"Remarkably clear, practical, and modern. An excellent feature
is the entrusting of each particular department of play to an acknowledged expert." - Birmingham Daily Post.
"Football now claims its handbooks, and will find one of the best in
the cheerful, breezy and manly production of Mr. Fletcher Robinson." - Daily Chronicle.
"All that is worth knowing about the game will be found
in this new volume." - Evening Citizen.

Evidently, BFR's first book was well received. Shortly after its publication, Max Pemberton was appointed editor of *Cassell's Family Magazine*. Consequently, he resigned the editorship of *The Isthmian Library* and that position passed to BFR. Between 1897 and 1901, BFR edited 8 volumes for *The Isthmian Library* and these included *Rowing* by R.C. Lehmann (see Plate 34). He also wrote 26 extended articles that were published by Pemberton (see Chapter 12) in *Cassell's Family Magazine* and *Cassell's Magazine* (see Plate 35). It should be noted that during 1897, Thomas Wemyss Reid was appointed manager of Cassell's Publishers and that *Cassell's Family Magazine* was subsequently renamed *Cassell's Magazine* after November 1897.

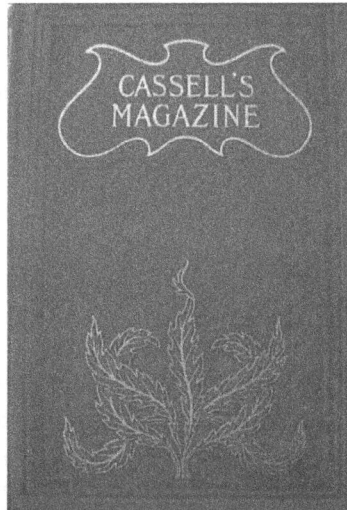

Plate 35. *Cassell's Magazine*
(December 1897 - May 1898).

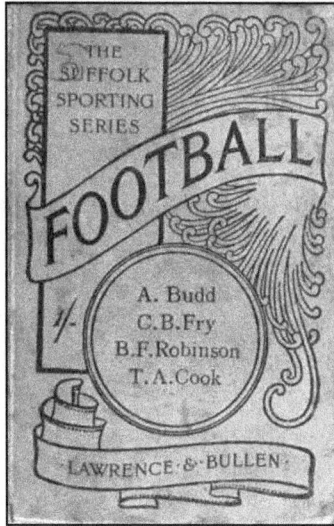

Plate 36. *Football* (1897)

In 1936, Pemberton referred to his relationship with BFR and other mutual acquaintances in an autobiography entitled *Sixty Years Ago and After* (London: Hutchinson & Company Publishers Limited). For example, he wrote that during 1897, BFR received an anonymous invitation to dine at the Reform Club. The same invitation card implored BFR not to disclose this engagement to his flatmate, Percy Illingworth. Meanwhile Illingworth had also received such an invitation and was instructed to conceal the appointment from BFR. Pemberton reported that BFR and Illingworth spent several uncomfortable days excusing themselves to one another ahead of their pending absence on a Wednesday night. The situation came to a head when each man tried to escape from their flat for the same covert destination using separate Hansom cabs. Eventually the two abashed men were reunited at the Reform Club where they were greeted by their anonymous host - an innocent looking Owen Seaman!

During March 1897, BFR had his first non-fictional article entitled *A Day with the Hounds* published in *Cassell's Family Magazine* (pp. 355-364). This article described the practice of riding-to-hounds with assorted provincial hunts. It is illustrated throughout with drawings by Jack Charlton and G. D. Armour and also with photographs. Both BFR and his father, Joseph Fletcher Robinson, were experienced huntsman and the theme is also referred to in a letter related to Sherlock Holmes by 'Dr.' James Mortimer in *The Hound of the Baskervilles*. In January 1899, *Cassell's Magazine* published a second related article that was written by BFR and entitled *The Duke's Hounds A Chat About The Badminton*.

On the 26th November 1897, it was announced in the *University Intelligence* column of *The Times* that a congregation had met at Cambridge University during the previous afternoon and had awarded BFR a Master of Arts degree. Several days later, BFR had the first in a series of six articles collectively entitled *Capitals at Play* published in the newly renamed *Cassell's Magazine*. This article was entitled *St. Petersburg* (pp. 18-29) and it is illustrated throughout with photographs (as are all of his articles in the series). This initial article is preceded by the following introduction:

> [Mr. B. Fletcher Robinson, the author of this
> remarkable series of articles, has just completed
> a tour of the capitals of Europe, solely in the

interests of CASSELL'S MAGAZINE. It has been his object to make himself familiar with the amusements of the various peoples concerned, and to show us the lighter side of life in the greater cities. With this object he has studied the pastimes of all classes indiscriminately. While he has not neglected the purely social, the more common recreations of the ordinary citizen have been his chief study. He shows us the people in their parks, their theatres, their gardens, and upon their rivers. The result, we venture to hope, is a series of articles which will be welcomed both by the old traveller and by those who have yet to visit the cities of which Mr. Robinson here treats.]

Max Pemberton reported in his autobiography that BFR had visited Livadia in the Crimea and was received by the entourage of Czar Nicholas II at The Old Grand Palace (later redeveloped and renamed The White Palace). BFR was entertained by the Emperor's Great Chamberlain and was subjected to persistent surveillance by the Russian Secret Police. It appears that BFR incorporated these experiences into a later work that was entitled *The Trail of the Dead – The Strange Experience of Dr. Robert Harland* (see Chapter 8).

On 27th November 1897, Lawrence and Bullen of London published a book entitled *Football* that was jointly written by one Arthur Budd and Charles Burgess Fry (see Plate 36). BFR also contributed to that same book, which was the 2nd in a series of volumes produced for *The Suffolk Sporting Series*. CB Fry was an Oxford Rugby Blue,

England cricketer and former world long-jump record holder. Budd was an ex-English rugby player and the brother of George Turnavine Budd, a Devon-based physician, who briefly employed ACD as a junior partner during 1882. George appears to have made a profound impression upon ACD because he features in two of his works thinly disguised as 'Dr. James Cullingworth'. The first of these books is entitled *The Stark Munro Letters* and was published by Longmans, Green and Company Limited in 1895. The second book is ACD's autobiography entitled *Memories and Adventures* that was first published as a serialisation in *The Strand Magazine* between October 1923 and July 1924.

Plate 37. Blackheath Football Club with Arthur Budd & Illingworth (stood 7th and 3rd from right respectively).
COURTESY OF THE PATRICK CASEY COLLECTION.

BERTRAM FLETCHER ROBINSON

Plate 38. *Rowing & Punting.*
© BRITISH LIBRARY BOARD. ALL RIGHTS RESERVED (7912.c76)

The association between BFR and Arthur Budd may have been rooted through their mutual acquaintance with Illingworth. Illingworth was at that time residing with BFR and both he and Arthur Budd were distinguished members of Blackheath Rugby Club in London. Each man had represented Blackheath 1st XV between 1887 and 1889 and Arthur Budd was elected club captain and president for the 1887/88 season. Arthur Budd and Illingworth feature together in the same team-photograph taken during the 1888/89 season (see Plate 37).

On 28th July 1898, Lawrence and Bullen of London published a book entitled *Rowing & Punting* that was jointly written by Douglas Hamilton McLean and William Henry Grenfell (see Plate 38). BFR also contributed to that same book, which was the 4th and final volume in the series produced for *The Suffolk Sporting Series on Sport* (see Plate 38). It was edited by Henry Charles Howard shortly

61

BERTRAM FLETCHER ROBINSON

before he died (18th Earl of Suffolk and 11th Earl of Berkshire). McLean was educated at Oxford University and was a quintuple Rowing Blue (1883/84/85/86/87). Grenfell was also educated at Oxford University and was a double Rowing Blue (1887/88) and former Amateur Punting Champion (1888/89/90).

During June 1899, *Cassell's Magazine* commenced publication of a series of six articles that were written by BFR and collectively entitled *London Night by Night*. In these articles, BFR outlined the high level of nocturnal activity that was required in order to meet the demands of Londoners for various services the following day. Each article is illustrated throughout with drawings by A. S. Hartrick and H. H. Flére. The first of these articles was numbered and entitled: *I. – The Next Day's Dinner* (pp. 48-56).

During July 1899, BFR had his first short story entitled *Black Magic: The Story of the Spanish Don*, published in *Cassell's Magazine* (pp. 178-189). It is illustrated throughout by F. H. Townsend. The story is narrated by an old Sailor (Jake) to an educated gentleman in a public house overlooking a Cornish harbour. Jake recalls meeting a strange Spanish-speaking passenger (the 'Don'), aboard a trading brig (the *Hampden*), during a voyage to Africa around 1856. It transpires that the 'Don' had recently murdered his friend for gold. The 'Don' becomes convinced that the murdered-man has possessed a shark, which is following the ship and is intent on exacting revenge against him. References to nautical terms, kerosene and palm oil, suggest that BFR may have adapted this story from tales told to him by his father.

Coincidentally, ACD worked as a Ship's physician aboard a West Africa bound cargo steamer called *S.S. Mayumba* between October 1881 and January 1882. During this trip, he contracted typhoid and almost died.

In December 1899, BFR had a non-fictional article numbered and entitled: *I. The Royal Horse Artillery*, published in *Cassell's Magazine* (pp. 121-129). It was the first of a continuous, six-part series collectively entitled *Famous Regiments* that was illustrated with photographs. One such photograph featured a famous painting by Richard Caton Woodville that is entitled *Saving the Guns at Maiwand* (see Plate 39).

Plate 39. *Saving the Guns at Maiwand* (1892).

BERTRAM FLETCHER ROBINSON

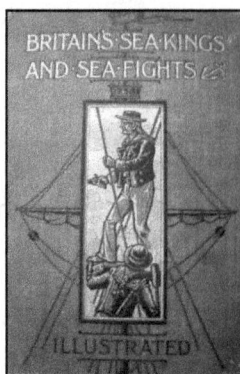

Plate 40. *Britain's Sea-Kings
and Sea-Fights* (1900).

The Battle of Maiwand, was fought in Afghanistan during 1880 and was at that time, the greatest defeat ever suffered by the British Army. This battle is referred to on the first page of the first Sherlock Holmes story, *A Study in Scarlet* (1887). It is interesting to note that Dr. Watson was wounded at the Battle of Maiwand and that this injury compelled him to retire from the Army and return to England, where he meets Sherlock Holmes. In his article on the Royal Horse Artillery, BFR mentions various places where the R.H.A. had acted courageously, and wrote:

> ...at Maiwand, where the men of E battery died at their guns, checking the wild rushes of the Ghazis, hot on the tracks of our shattered force...

A member of E Battery called Sergeant Mullane, won the Victoria Cross at Maiwand for picking up a wounded

Gunner and carrying him, under fire, to safety. ACD, in the guise of Dr Watson, wrote:

> I served at the fatal battle of Maiwand. There I was struck on the shoulder by a Jezail bullet, which shattered the bone and grazed the sub-clavian artery. I should have fallen into the hands of the murderous Ghazis had it not been for the devotion and courage shown by Murray, my orderly, who threw me across a packhorse, and succeeded in bringing me safely to the British lines.

It is an interesting to note that there was a survivor of E Battery, Gunner Loosemore, who was wounded at the Battle of Maiwand and forced to return to England. Following his retirement from the Army in the 1880's, Loosemore resided in Exeter, whilst BFR lived in nearby Ipplepen (20 miles or 32 kilometres).

On 25th January 1900, Cassell and Company Limited published a 760-page non-fictional book entitled *Britain's Sea-Kings and Sea-Fights* (see Plate 40). This book was written by various authors and they are listed as follows: BFR, Commander Claud Harding R.N., Tighe Hopkins, F. Norreys Connell, Captain H. Garbett R.N., Herbert Compton, Major Le Mesurier Gretton, A. Hilliard Atteridge and others. BFR contributed 4 of the 35 chapters, as follows:

BERTRAM FLETCHER ROBINSON

I. *The Beginnings of the British Navy, from the Days of Alfred the Great to the Days of Good Queen Bess* (pp. 1-38).

II. *The Early Exploits of Francis Drake* (pp. 39-60).

VIII. *From the Armada to the Great Rebellion* (pp. 149-200).

XIII. *How Europe Fought for the Spanish Crown* (pp. 329-358).

The book is illustrated throughout with numerous reproductions of famous pictures, old prints, plans, trophies and relics. Additional artwork was supplied by various illustrators including Walter Paget (affectionately referred to as 'Wal'). It is interesting to note that Walter Paget was chosen to illustrate the serialized version of *The Adventures of Sherlock Holmes* that ran in *The Strand Magazine* between July 1891 and December 1892. However, the letter of commission was sent in error to Walter's older brother, Sidney Paget. In total, Sidney produced 356 Holmes' illustrations, including 60 for *The Hound of the Baskervilles*. It has been suggested that Sidney used Walter as a model for Holmes' physical appearance (see Plates 41 & 42).

Plate 41. Walter Paget

Plate 42. Sherlock Holmes by Sidney Paget.

Chapter 5

South Africa

During the late 1880s, gold was discovered in the independent Boer republic of the Transvaal. At about that same time, Britain's gold reserves were depleting and many British citizens travelled to the Transvaal to engage in prospecting. The Boer Government, headed by President Paul Kruger, tried to prevent the influx of foreign prospectors by limiting their voting rights. This angered many colonists including the British High Commissioner for South Africa, Sir Alfred Milner. He made comments that both stirred British imperialistic feeling and angered Boer republicans. By late September 1899, reconciliation talks between Milner and Kruger had failed. On 11th October 1899, the British held Natal and Cape Colonies in South Africa were invaded by neighbouring Boers from the Orange Free State and Transvaal Province. This was the first action of the 2nd Boer War (1899-1902).

Between 10th December 1899 and 15th December 1899, the republicans inflicted a series of three defeats upon the British Army. In Britain, the news of 'Black Week' triggered public alarm and a demand for more news from the front lines. This climate prompted the publisher Cyril Arthur Pearson (see Plate 43) to plan the introduction of a new daily newspaper. However, in order to do this and retain both *Pearson's Weekly* and *Pearson's Magazine* (see Plate 44), he required more staff. Meanwhile, BFR's series of articles entitled *Famous Regiments* had commenced publication in *Cassell's Magazine* (December 1899 – May

1900). Moreover, he was the principle contributor to *Britain's Sea-Kings and Sea-Fights* that was published on 25th January 1900. It appears that Pearson was impressed by this work because he subsequently employed BFR as a journalist and assigned him to write about military matters in South Africa (see Plate 45).

Plate 43.
Cyril Arthur Pearson.
COURTESY OF THE TOPFOTO COLLECTION

Plate 44.
Pearson's Magazine
(January - June 1900).

On 24th December 1899, 40 year-old ACD tried to enlist in the Middlesex Yeomanry but the military authorities rejected him because of his age and general condition. ACD subsequently accepted an offer to work as 'senior civil surgeon' for his friend, John Langman. The latter man planned to open a field hospital at Bloemfontein, the then capital of the Orange Free State. Shortly thereafter, ACD commenced writing a book that was later entitled *The Great Boer War*. On 28th February 1900, ACD departed from the Port of Tilbury in Essex for Cape Town in South Africa aboard the P&O steamship, *Oriental*.

Plate 45. BFR (circa 1900).
COURTESY OF THE TOPFOTO COLLECTION.

During March 1901, BFR had a short non-fictional article entitled *A True Story – Being the Adventure of Certain Golf Players* published in both the British and American editions of *Pearson's Magazine*. This was the first of 26 fictional and non-fictional items that BFR had published or republished in the two editions of that periodical over the course of the next 4½ years. This article is interesting in so far that BFR and ACD conceived the idea for *The Hound of the Baskervilles* during a golfing holiday at Cromer during April 1901 (see Chapter 6). BFR's contributions to the British edition of *Pearson's Magazine* also included 2 articles entitled *The Hunting of the Fox* (January 1902) and *Historic Monuments of Britain. III. The Fortress of the First Britons. A Description of the Fortress of Grimspound, on Dartmoor* (see Chapter 7).

In mid-March 1900, BFR also departed England for Cape Town by ship. It appears from advertisements placed in

The Times newspaper that BFR was assigned by Pearson to work as part of a small group of 'War Correspondents' (see Plate 46). This group reported on a range of war-related matters and their dispatches were subsequently published as articles in Pearson's nascent *Daily Express* newspaper. This periodical was billed as a 'New Morning London Newspaper' and the first edition appeared on 24th April 1900. It was the first British daily newspaper to print news on its front page.

PEARSON'S NEW ½D. MORNING PAPER
DAILY EXPRESS
Will have an unrivalled organization for collecting news. It has seven War Correspondents in South Africa, and has appointed its Own Special Correspondents in all centres of any importance. So far as British interests are concerned the Paper has its Own Representative in every town in the British Empire.

Plate 46. Part of an advertisement for the *Daily Express* that appeared in *The Times* newspaper (23rd April 1900).

On 21st March 1900, ACD arrived in South Africa and he resided at The Mount Nelson Hotel in Cape Town (see Plate 47). That same hotel was frequently used by statesman and senior military figures to discuss war strategy. Previous guests had included Lords Kitchener, Buller and Roberts. The Mount Nelson Hotel had also been used by a 25 year-old British journalist and future prime minister, Winston Churchill.

On 26th March 1900, ACD departed Cape Town for East London in the Eastern Cape Province. This was the only river port in South Africa, and he arrived there 2 days later. ACD then proceeded by train to Bloemfontein and helped to set-up The Langman Hospital that opened on 2nd April (see Plate 48). During the next 2½ months, ACD treated many patients (see Plate 49) and continued writing his book about the 2nd Boer War.

Plate 47. The Mount Nelson Hotel
(circa 1938).

During April 1900, BFR arrived at Cape Town and also resided at The Mount Nelson Hotel. On 3rd April, he attended a pro-British rally at Cape Town House in Green Market Square. The crowd of 10,000-15,000 people repeatedly sang the *God Save the Queen* and *Rule Britannia*. This rally was addressed by various speakers including the Mayor of Cape Town, Colonel Robert Baden Powell and Sir John Gordon Sprigg (Prime Minister of the Cape Colony). The following day, BFR sent his 1st dispatch to the offices of the *Daily Express*. It was subsequently published by that newspaper on 4th May 1900 under the title *Capetown for Empire*. In this item, BFR made the following comments in relation to Sprigg's speech:

"Put on your hat, sir," we shouted, for it is dangerous playing tricks with the South African sun. But Sir Gordon had a ready answer for us. "I can stand here without my hat," he shouted, "so long as I am protected by the flag that waves above me." How we cheered! He had to pause for a good two minutes.

On 17th April 1900, BFR sent a 2nd and less triumphant dispatch from Cape Town. It was subsequently published in the *Daily Express* on 8th May 1900 under the title *In a Cape Hotel*. In this item, BFR reports upon a conversation that he had with an officer from the 'Irregular Horse' at The Mount Nelson Hotel. The soldier was returning to Cape Town to procure fresh kit for his squadron following an ambush by Boer republicans at Bloemfontein Waterworks. BFR quotes the soldier as stating that in the aftermath of that attack, there had been 'fifteen hundred cases' of enteric (typhoid) at Bloemfontein. On 20th April 1900, ACD wrote a letter to his mother and stated that 'I have 50 enteric cases to look after'. He also wrote in his diary that 'One man died as I fanned him. I saw the light go out of his eyes.'

During 1900, ACD had a paper entitled *The Epidemic of Enteric Fever in Bloemfontein* published in *The British Medical Journal* (No. 2, pp. 49-50). In this item, ACD reports 600 deaths at Bloemfontein in just one month! During 1900, only 10 per cent of the British troops in South Africa were inoculated for typhoid, even though Almroth Wright had developed a vaccine four years earlier. ACD observed that there had been no deaths among inoculated patients in a period of 1 month. Later, ACD wrote in his autobiography that 'We lost more from the enteric than from the bullet in South Africa'.

Plate 48. The Langman Hospital.

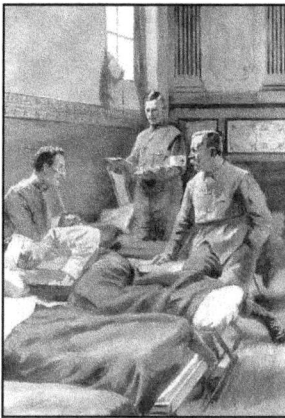

Plate 49. ACD treating patients
at The Langman Hospital.

On 8th May 1900, BFR sent an 8th dispatch from Cape Town. It was subsequently published by the *Daily Express* on 26th May under the title *Behind the Veil*. This article reports a chance encounter between BFR and a train driver called Richard Booth. The latter man was injured by Boer fighters in the Transvaal and subsequently imprisoned in Pretoria. BFR also writes that Booth was originally from Newton Abbot '...near which town I also live, we fraternized with much hand shaking'. This statement is important for two reasons. Firstly it implies that after completing the Bar Examination in April 1896, BFR split his time between residing with Lewis and Illingworth in London and his parents in Devon. Secondly, it reveals that by that time, BFR considered himself to be a Devonian.

On 8th May 1900, BFR also sent a 9th dispatch from Cape Town. It was subsequently published by the *Daily Express* on 29th May under the title *Nursing an Army*. In this item, BFR comments upon the logistical difficulties experienced by the Army Service Corps in maintaining supplies to British led forces. He illustrates this by reference to the single railway by which, all medical supplies for fighting dysentery and enteric were being sent to Bloemfontein. Interestingly, ACD suffered from dysentery whilst serving there and it also appears that he experienced a mild relapse of enteric despite having been inoculated for it. Ironically, it took him 10 years to fully recover, by which time BFR had himself died from the disease in London (see Chapter 9).

On 15th May 1900, BFR sent a 10th dispatch from Cape Town. It was subsequently published by the *Daily Express* on 7th June 1900 under the title *Real Nurses or Mere*

Trippers. In this article, BFR refers to a trip that he made during the previous month to the nearby Woodstock Military Hospital. He states that there was just 1 volunteer nurse to 70 beds and that the orderlies had no previous experience. He also reports that each day, there was between 4 and 6 military funerals conducted at that hospital. BFR attacks the criticism aimed at the volunteer nursing staff working under such conditions by people such as Sir Alfred Milner. Later, ACD wrote the following related comments in his autobiography about the conduct of volunteer nurses during the height of the enteric epidemic at Bloemfontein:

> ...two nursing sisters appeared among us, and never shall I forget what angels of light they appeared, or how they nursed those poor boys, swaddling them like babies and meeting every want with gentle courage. Thank God, they both came through safe.

On 6th June 1900, BFR sent a 12th and 13th dispatch from Graaf-Reinert in the Eastern Cape (these were his last 2 dispatches from South Africa). The first of these was subsequently published by the *Daily Express* on 25th June under the title *How I nearly Became A Rebel*. The second was published by that same newspaper on 30th June under the title *How the Bond Promotes Peace*. In these items, BFR describes the events surrounding a rally at Graaf-Reinert (31st May 1900) that was addressed by a Pro-Boer Englishman called Ernest Temple Hargrove. During that journey, BFR shared a railway compartment with a Boer rebel and 2 prominent Bondsmen. The Bond was a political organisation that opposed British military action in

South Africa at that time. The Bondsmen behaved in a courteous manner towards BFR but the rebel persistently mocked the British. BFR challenged him to 'step outside at the next station' but upon arrival, the Boer was nowhere to be seen.

On 11th July 1900, both BFR and ACD departed Cape Town for England aboard the steamship, *Briton* (see Plate 50). The pair shared a dining table and they were photographed together (see Plate 51). ACD wrote in his autobiography that it was during this voyage that he 'cemented' his friendship with BFR. This statement might imply that they had met previously, perhaps at the Reform Club in London, to which both men belonged. ACD also recalled that during the voyage, a French Army officer called Major Roger Raoul Duval accused the British of using dum-dum bullets during the 2nd Boer War campaign. ACD reacted angrily to this allegation and BFR helped to reconcile the dispute. BFR's solicitor friend, Harold Gaye Michelmore, (see Chapter 2), later reported in a letter published in *The Western Morning News* that during that same voyage:

> ...Fletcher Robinson told Doyle the plot of the story which he intended writing about Dartmoor, and Conan Doyle was so intrigued by it that he asked Fletcher Robinson if he would object to their writing it together.

> It may be interesting to recall that during the same voyage Fletcher Robinson asked Conan Doyle if it had occurred to him how easy it would be to implicate a man in a murder crime

if you could obtain a finger-print of his in wax for reproduction in blood on a wall or some other obvious place near the seat of the crime.

Conan Doyle was taken by the idea and asked Fletcher Robinson whether he intended to use it in his own literary work. Fletcher Robinson replied: "not immediately," and Conan Doyle offered him 50 pounds for the idea which Fletcher Robinson accepted, and Conan Doyle incorporated the idea in one of the Sherlock Holmes tales which he published shortly afterwards.

Hence it appears that BFR and ACD agreed to co-author a Dartmoor-based story during their voyage aboard the *S.S. Briton*. However, it is unlikely that 'the story' bore much resemblance to *The Hound of the Baskervilles* (see Chapter 6). Perhaps, 'the story' to which Michelmore referred was one of two other Dartmoor-linked stories that BFR wrote after the various versions of *The Hound of the Baskervilles* were printed (1901/02)? The first of these was a fairy-tale entitled *The Battle of Fingle's Bridge* that was published during May 1903 in *Pearson's Magazine* (Vol. 15, pp. 530-536). The second was a short story entitled *The Mystery of Thomas Hearne* that features as the 5th chapter of his 1905 book, *The Chronicles of Addington Peace* (London: Harper & Brother). ACD subsequently used BFR's fingerprint idea in a Sherlock Holmes story entitled *The Adventure of the Norwood Builder* that was first published in *Collier's Weekly Magazine* (1903). This was the 2nd of 32 Holmes short stories that he wrote after the publication of *The Hound of the Baskervilles*.

Plate 50. *S.S. Briton.*
COURTESY OF THE TOPFOTO COLLECTION.

Plate 51. BFR (seated centre) and ACD (behind his left
shoulder) aboard the *S.S. Briton* (July 1900).

79

BERTRAM FLETCHER ROBINSON

On 28th July 1900, the *S.S. Briton* docked at Southampton on the southern coast of England. Thereafter, BFR returned to live with Lewis and Illingworth at 126 Ashley Gardens in London and he was promoted to 'debut-editor' of the *Daily Express*. On 23rd October 1900, ACD's book entitled *The Great Boer War* was published by Smith, Elder & Company of London. BFR also continued to write about the 2nd Boer War in columns 4-7 of the London News section of the *Daily Express*. Between August 1900 and June 1904, BFR had a further 87 by-lined articles published and 9 of these items relate to events in South Africa.

During early 1901, Sir John Robinson retired as manager and editor of the London *Daily News* and BFR's friend, Rudolph Lehmann, was appointed to replace him. BFR's flatmate, Percy Illingworth, returned to the West Riding of Yorkshire to live with his family at Lady Royde Hall. Thereafter, BFR also departed 126 Ashley Gardens and he relocated to the home of his uncle, Sir John Robinson at 4 Addison Crescent, Kensington, London (see Plate 52). Thus only Trevor Lewis remained in residence at 126 Ashley Gardens.

On 21st May 1901, the *Daily Express* published an article that was written by BFR and entitled *Truthful Jean' on the War*. In this item, BFR reviewed an autobiographical account of the 2nd Boer War entitled *La Guerre Transvaal – En Pleine Epopée* ('The Transvaal War – At the Height of the Epic'). The book's author, Jean Carreres, is generally critical of British foreign policy towards the Boers, but is

Plate 52. 4 Addison Crescent where BFR lived with his uncle, Sir John Robinson between 1901 and 1902.

complimentary about ACD, a point that BFR emphasised as follows:

> "What a man!" cried the enthusiastic Frenchman; "and what a brave man! How his merciful and thoughtful words consoled me after the foolish rodomontades [pretentious boasting or bragging] I had listened to!" "He ought to write a book on the war" – M. Carrere was gifted with a spirit of prophecy – "I do not know if in his style and in the impression his adventures left on him he will be better or worse than Kipling; but I am certain that he will be more humane – more impartial. He loves and defends the English soldier, but he understands the spirit of the Boer, and it is in that the secret of justice lies."

BERTRAM FLETCHER ROBINSON

Carreres was a correspondent for the French newspaper, *Le Matin*. It appears that ACD met with him at the Transvaal Hotel in Pretoria during late June 1900. Interestingly, ACD later used the name 'Carere' for one of the minor characters in *The Hound of the Baskervilles*. BFR's review of Carreres' book also reveals that he read French.

On 16th January 1902, ACD elaborated upon his views about the 2nd Boer War in a sixpenny pamphlet entitled *The War in South Africa - Its Cause and Conduct*. This work was seemingly prompted by public unease over foreign reports of alleged British atrocities and the use of concentration camps. ACD did not condone the conditions in such camps, but he argued that there was a need to isolate guerrilla Boers from sympathetic homestead families. Such defence of British policy in layman terms won him unprecedented public acclaim. On 24th October 1902, ACD was both knighted and appointed a Deputy Lieutenant of Surrey by King Edward VII at Buckingham Palace.

On 31st May 1902, the 2nd Boer War concluded with the signing of the *Treaty of Vereeniging*. It awarded reconstruction costs and the promise of self-government to the Orange Free State and the South African Republic in return for incorporation into the British Empire. It is estimated that the 2nd Boer War claimed some 75,000 lives; 22,000 British soldiers (7,792 battle casualties, the rest through disease), 6,000-7,000 Boer soldiers, 20,000-28,000 Boer civilians and perhaps 20,000 native Africans.

Chapter 6

The Hound of the Baskervilles

Plate 53. *Åsgårdsreien* (or 'Wild Hunt')
by Peter Nicolai Arbo (1872).

BFR wrote that he lived in Ipplepen whilst working for the *Daily Express* in South Africa. It is therefore reasonable to assume that he returned there to see his parents shortly after returning to England on 28th July 1900. The following month, the annual meeting of the Devonshire Association was held at Totnes in Devon (some 5 miles from Ipplepen). During that meeting, the *17th Report of the Committee on Devonshire Folk-Lore* was presented to the assembled membership. Later that same year, it was published in the *Report and Transactions of the Devonshire Association* (Vol. XXXII, pp. 83-84). Given that Joseph Fletcher Robinson was a member of the Devonshire Association (1884-1903), it is likely that BFR read the following entry from that periodical:

BERTRAM FLETCHER ROBINSON

Wish or Yeth Hounds. – Mr. Hardinge F. Giffard sends a valuable addition to our scanty information respecting the belief in these weird Dartmoor spectres. The late Mr. R. J. King, in an article on Dartmoor, writing of Wistman's Wood, remarked-

The name of the wood connects it with the form in which the widely-held belief in the 'wild hunter' is known on Dartmoor. The cry of the *whish* or *whished* hounds is heard occasionally in the loneliest recesses of the hills, whilst neither dogs nor huntsmen are anywhere visible. At other times (generally on a Sunday) they show themselves jet-black, breathing flames, and followed by a tall, swart figure, who carries a hunting pole. Wisc or Wish, according to Kemble, was a name of Woden, the lord of 'wish,' who is probably represented by the master of these dogs of darkness."- Quarterly Review, July, 1873.

Mr. Hardinge Giffard writes: "In 1886 or 1887, while staying for a few days in the parish of Hittisleigh (a hilly parish of scattered houses, about 8 miles W.S.W. of Crediton in Devon), I met an elderly man, whose name was, I think, Hill, from whom I endeavored to elicit some information concerning the pixies. Reluctant at first to speak on the subject, Mr. Hill, having apparently satisfied himself that my interest was genuine, told me that his father, who had died a very old man, firmly believed in the existence of the wish or yeth hounds. This belief was based on his experience, which, as told by his son, was as follows. Mr. Hill, senior, was at one time employed at the stables at Oaklands, Okehampton, now the property of General Holley. Late one evening, when the horses had been groomed by himself and others, he heard what he believed to be a pack of hounds in full cry at no great distance. Leaving the stables, Mr. Hill ran out and distinctly heard the sound of a horn and the cry of hounds on the moor (Dartmoor) close at hand. Astonished and frightened, he returned to the stables, only to find the horses, which he had left cool and comfortable, trembling with fear and covered with sweat. My informant assured me that his father swore to the truth of his statement, and ever afterwards was a firm believer in the wish hounds, which are popularly supposed to haunt the vicinity of Dartmoor on certain nights in the year, more especially on St. John's Eve [23rd June]. Without actually admitting it in so many words, my informant obviously inherited his father's belief. I should add that Mr. Hill assured me that it was established beyond doubt that no pack of hounds in the flesh had been anywhere in the

neighbourhood on the night in question."
H.F.G.

Readers of *The Hound of the Baskervilles* will note
parallels between this entry and that of the 'Baskerville
Legend' that is communicated to Sherlock Holmes by
Mortimer. The reference to Woden, the English Anglo-
Saxon God of wisdom, is particularly striking because he is
frequently portrayed in folklore as the leader of a 'Wild
Hunt' (see Plate 53). Such myths entail a mad pursuit
across the sky by phantasmal huntsmen with horses and
hounds. In many Scandinavian and German versions, the
hunt is often for a woman, who is captured or killed. It is
notable that in the 'Baskerville Legend', a Yeoman's
daughter dies of fear and fatigue after fleeing across
Dartmoor from a pack of hunting hounds that is led by her
kidnapper, 'wicked Hugo Baskerville'. Interestingly,
Woden is also known by many other names including
'Grim'. This name was integrated into the fictitious
settings of 'Grimpen' and 'the great Grimpen Mire' in *The
Hound of the Baskervilles*.

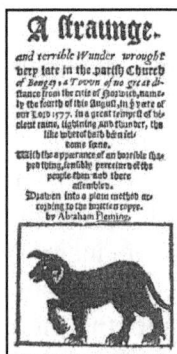

Plate 54. Black Shuck by Abraham Fleming (1577).

BERTRAM FLETCHER ROBINSON

During late April 1901, 30 year-old BFR dined at the London home of his friend and former editor, Max Pemberton (see Chapter 4). At that time, 37 year-old Pemberton was working as an author and was residing with his wife and family at 56 Fitzjohn's Avenue, Hampstead. During dinner, Pemberton related a story about a large, solitary hound, with glowing eyes that reportedly terrorised the coastline of Norfolk. In some tales, this hound, called Black Shuck (see Plate 54), would ascend from the beach at Cromer to nearby Cromer Hall on a path that took it past the Royal Links Hotel (see Plate 55). On 25th May 1939, the London *Evening News* published the following account of Sir Max Pemberton's recollection of that dinner with BFR:

> The late Fletcher Robinson who collaborated, with Doyle in the story, was dining at my house in Hampstead one night when the talk turned upon phantom dogs. I told my friend of a certain Jimmy Farman, a Norfolk marshman, who swore that there was a phantom dog on the marshes near St. Olives [near Great Yarmouth, Norfolk] and that his bitch had met the brute more than once and had been terrified by it. 'A Great black dog it were,' Jimmy said, 'and the eyes of 'un was like railway lamps. He crossed my path down there by the far dyke and the old bitch a'most went mad wi' fear…Now surely that bitch saw a' summat I didn't see…'

> Fletcher Robinson assured me that dozens of people on the outskirts of Dartmoor had seen a

phantom hound and that to doubt its existence would be a local heresy. In both instances, the brute was a huge retriever, coal black and with eyes which shone like fire.

Fletcher Robinson was always a little psychic and he had a warm regard for this apparition; indeed, he expressed some surprise that no romancer had yet written about it. Three nights afterwards, Fletcher Robinson was dining with Sir [sic] Arthur. The talk at my house was still fresh in his mind and he told Doyle what I had said, emphasising that this particular marshman was as sure of the existence of the phantom hound as he was of his own being. Finally, Fletcher Robinson said 'Let us write the story together.' And to his great content Sir [sic] Arthur cordially assented."

Between Friday 26th April 1901 and Monday 29th April 1901, BFR and ACD stayed at the Royal Links Hotel in Cromer. ACD hoped that this golfing weekend might speed his recovery from the illness that he had contracted in South Africa. However, it is unlikely that ACD and BFR played many rounds of golf because local weather records reveal that the weekend was generally overcast, damp, cold and breezy (the mean daily temperature and wind-speed were 7°C and 20.7mph). Instead, it appears that BFR entertained ACD with tales of the 'Wild Hunt' on Dartmoor and Black Shuck. During April 1902, a journalist called John Earnest Hodder-Williams wrote the following account of that trip to Cromer for a British periodical called *The Bookman* (London):

Robinson is a Devonshire man [sic], and he mentioned in conversation some old-country legend which set Doyle's imagination on fire. The two men began building up a chain of events, and in a very few hours the plot for a sensational story was conceived and it was agreed that Doyle should write it.

On Sunday 28th April, ACD sent a letter to his mother from Cromer in which, he stated that "Fletcher Robinson came here with me and we are going to do a small book together 'The Hound of the Baskervilles' – a real creeper." He also wrote a second letter to Herbert Greenhough Smith (see Plate 56), the editor of *The Strand Magazine*, in which, he again described the story as a 'real creeper'. ACD offered Greenhough Smith the story but insisted that, 'I must do it with my friend Robinson and his name must appear with mine'. He added, 'I shall want my usual 50 pounds per thousand words for all rights if you do business'.

Plate 55. Royal Links Hotel at Cromer (circa 1900).

Plate 56. Herbert G. Smith.

During early May 1901, ACD decided that the book needed some masterful central figure and reflected, 'Why should I invent such a character when I have him already in the form of Sherlock Holmes?' ACD subsequently contacted Greenhough Smith and offered him a second version of the same story, a version that would incorporate Holmes. Greenhough Smith agreed to pay £100 per thousand words to ACD for the Holmes version.

Plate 57. The Revd R. D. Cooke.
COURTESY OF WENDY MAJOR.

Plate 58. Duchy Hotel (1905).
PHOTOGRAPH BY DAVID GERMAN.

By mid-may 1901, the 1st instalment of *The Hound of the Baskervilles* (Chapters I-II of XV) had arrived at the offices of *The Strand Magazine*. Records made by Sidney Paget, reveal that he was paid £34 13s. at the end of May for completing 7 illustrations to accompany this 1st

instalment. This would have been impossible if Paget had not first read the instalment during that month. On Saturday 25th May 1901, the following announcement appeared in *Tit-Bits*. This periodical was, like *The Strand Magazine*, also published by George Newnes:

The Revival of Sherlock Holmes

Very many readers of The Strand Magazine have asked us over and over again if we could not induce Mr. Conan Doyle to give us some more stories of this wonderful character. Mr. Conan Doyle has been engaged on other work, but presently he will give us an important story to appear in the Strand, in which the great Sherlock Holmes is the principle character. It will appear in both the British and American editions. In America the play founded upon the career of the great detective has run for many months with enormous success. It is going to be produced in London in about three months, and at the same time the new Sherlock Holmes story will commence in the Strand. It will be published as a serial of from 30,000 to 50,000 words, and the plot is one of the most interesting and striking that have [sic] ever been put before us. We are sure that all those readers of the Strand who have written to us on the matter, and those who have not, will be very glad that Mr. Conan Doyle is going to give us some more about our old favourite [sic].

BERTRAM FLETCHER ROBINSON

Evidently, BFR was content for the story to be published under ACD's name alone because he willingly undertook two related research trips to Dartmoor during May 1901. The first of these took place in the company of his friend, The Revd Robert Duins Cooke (see Plate 57). He was the vicar of St. Andrew's Church in Ipplepen where Joseph Fletcher Robinson had been acting as churchwarden for 18 years. In a letter published on the 9th February 1949 by *The Western Morning News*, The Revd Henry Robert Cooke reported the following:

> Sir – May I add to Mr. H. G. Michelmore's interesting letter on "The Hound of the Baskervilles." My father – Prebendary R. D. Cooke – was Vicar of Ipplepen at the date you mention, 1901. He was a great authority on Dartmoor. Mr. B. F. Robinson asked his advice and help in planning the background of his story.
>
> My father and Mr. Robinson went up to the Moor together, and under my father's guidance the details of the background were filled in on the spot! My father was very proud of this and often told his children how he had helped to write a very well known book.
>
> My sister, Mrs. Graeme, of Shaldon, has a copy of the book presented to my father by Mr. B. F. Robinson, and inscribed: "To Rev. R. D. Cooke from the assistant plot producer, Bertram Fletcher Robinson."

BERTRAM FLETCHER ROBINSON

Between Friday 31st May 1901 and Sunday 2nd June 1901, BFR made a second research trip to Dartmoor in the company of ACD. The two men stayed at the Duchy Hotel at Princetown (see Plate 58). It was owned by 52 year-old Aaron Rowe (see Plate 59), and staffed by three of his daughters and two of his sisters. ACD and BFR were accompanied on this trip by a 30 year-old coachman called Henry Baskerville (see Plate 60) who was employed by Joseph Fletcher Robinson. 'Harry' shared the same Christian and surname as a central character within the story of *The Hound of the Baskervilles*.

Plate 59. Aaron Rowe.

BERTRAM FLETCHER ROBINSON

Plate 60. Henry Baskerville (coachman).
COURTESY OF WENDY MAJOR.

On Saturday 1 June 1901, ACD wrote a letter to his mother from the Duchy Hotel (see overleaf). This letter is important for two reasons. Firstly, it records his initial impression to the area about Princetown. Secondly, it states that he intended to visit Park Hill House at Ipplepen. Other sources confirm that ACD did indeed play in all the cricket matches as listed. Hence, there is little reason to doubt that he also made the intended journey to Ipplepen. At that time, the shortest route between Princetown and Ipplepen was a 4-hour drive that incorporated Hexworthy, Holne, Buckfastleigh, Ashburton and Denbury. This meant that ACD must have departed Devon for Sherborne on either the evening of 2 June or morning of 3 June.

BERTRAM FLETCHER ROBINSON

Dearest of Mams

Here I am in the highest town in England. Robinson and I are exploring the moor together over our Sherlock Holmes book. I think it will work splendidly – indeed I have already done nearly half of it. Holmes is at his very best, and it is a highly dramatic idea which I owe to Robinson.

We did 14 miles over the Moor today and we are now pleasantly weary. It is a great place, very sad & wild, dotted with the dwellings of prehistoric man, strange monoliths and huts and graves. In those old days there was evidently a population of very many thousands here & now you may walk all day and never see one human being. Everywhere there are gutted tin mines. Tomorrow [Sunday 2nd June] we drive 16 miles to Ipplepen where R's parents live. Then on Monday Sherborne for the cricket, 2 days at Bath, 2 days at Cheltenham. Home on Monday 10th. That is my programme.

A trip to Buckfastleigh would have enabled BFR to show ACD both the former home and possible grave of Squire Richard Cabell III (see Plates 61 & 62). An entry in *The House of Commons Journal* for 1647, reports that the squire was fined by Parliament for siding with the Royalists in the English Civil War. Later, he retracted his support for King Charles I and was pardoned. Undoubtedly, this act angered local people who depended upon The Duchy of Cornwall for their livelihood. Perhaps for this reason, malicious stories about the squire abounded. In one such story, he reputedly accused his wife of adultery and a struggle ensued. She fled to nearby Dartmoor but he recaptured and murdered her with his hunting knife. The victim's pet hound exacted revenge by ripping out the squire's throat and some say that its anguished howls can still be heard at night. In reality, Cabell's wife actually outlived her husband by 14 years but the legend nevertheless persisted. Again, there are parallels between this story and the legend of the 'wicked Hugo Baskerville' in *The Hound of the Baskervilles*. Later, Holmes solved the case when he noticed a resemblance between a 1647 portrait of Hugo dressed as a Royalist and another character called Stapleton. It is possible that this part of the 'Baskerville Legend' was suggested by BFR, who held qualifications in both history and law.

Plate 61. Brook Manor at West Buckfastleigh (southern façade).
PHOTOGRAPH BY ANTHONY HOWLETT ©1992.

BERTRAM FLETCHER ROBINSON

Plate 62. The sepulchre built for Squire Richard Cabell III (located by the Holy Trinity Church porch, Buckfastleigh).

On 26th November 1905, a Californian born journalist called Henry Jackson Wells Dam published an article entitled *Arthur Conan Doyle – An Appreciation of the Author of 'Sir Nigel', the Great Romance Which Begins Next Sunday*, in the *Sunday Magazine* supplement of *The New York Tribune*. This article included an account of BFR's recollections about his trip to Dartmoor with ACD:

> One of the most interesting weeks that I have ever spent was with Doyle on Dartmoor. He made the journey in my company shortly after I told him, and he had accepted from me, a plot which eventuated in the 'Hound of the Baskervilles'. Dartmoor, the great wilderness of bog and rock that cuts Devonshire at this point, appealed to his imagination. He listened eagerly to my stories of ghost hounds, of the headless riders and of the devils that lurk in the hollows – legends upon which I have been reared, for my

98

home lay on the boarders of the moor. How well he turned to account his impressions will be remembered by all readers of 'The Hound'.

Two incidents come especially to my recollection. In the centre of the moor lies the famous convict prison of Princetown. In the great granite buildings, swept by the rains and clouded in the mists, are lodged over a thousand criminals, convicted on the more serious offences. A tiny village clusters at the foot of the slope on which they stand, and a comfortable old-fashioned inn affords accommodation to travellers.

The morning after our arrival Doyle and I were sitting in the smoking-room when a cherry-cheeked maid opened the door and announced 'Visitors to see you, gentlemen' [probably one of Aaron Rowe's daughters]. In marched four men, who solemnly sat down and began to talk about the weather, the fishing in the moor streams and other general subjects. Who they might be I had not the slightest idea. As they left I followed them into the hall of the inn. On the table were their four cards. The governor of the prison, the deputy governor, the chaplain and the doctor had come [William Russell, Cyril Platt, Lawrence Hudson and William Frew respectively], as a pencil note explained, 'to call on Mr. Sherlock Holmes.'

One morning I took Doyle to see the mighty bog [Fox Tor Mires], a thousand acres of quaking slime, at any part of which a horse and rider might disappear, which figured so prominently in *The Hound.* He was amused at the story I told him of the moor man who on one occasion saw a hat near the edge of the morass and poked at it with a long pole he carried. 'You leave my hat alone!' came a voice from beneath it. 'Whoi'! Be there a man under 'at?' cried the startled rustic. 'Yes, you fool, and a horse under the man.'

From the bog we tramped eastward to the stone fort of Grimspound, which the savages of the Stone Age in Britain, the aborigines who were earlier settlers than Saxons or Danes or Norsemen, raised with enormous labour to act as a haven of refuge from marauding tribes to the South. The good preservation in which the Grimspound fort still remains is marvellous. The twenty-feet slabs of granite – how they were ever hauled to their places is a mystery to historian and engineer – still encircle the stone huts where the tribe lived. Into one of these Doyle and I walked, and sitting down on the stone which probably served the three thousand year-old chief as a bed we talked of the races of the past. It was one of the loneliest spots in Great Britain. No road came within a long distance of the place. Strange legends of lights and figures are told concerning it. Add thereto that it was a gloomy day overcast with heavy cloud.

Suddenly we heard a boot strike against a stone without and rose together. It was only a lonely tourist on a walking excursion, but at sight of our heads suddenly emerging from the hut he let out a yell and bolted. Our subsequent disappearance was due to the fact that we both sat down and rocked with laughter, and as he did not return I have small doubt Mr. Doyle and I added yet another proof of the supernatural to tellers of ghost stories concerning Dartmoor.

Evidently, these experiences impressed ACD because he subsequently incorporated a bog called 'the great Grimpen Mire' and an ancient stone hut into the plot of *The Hound of the Baskervilles*. Furthermore, on Thursday 13th June 1901, less than two weeks after he met the four senior officials from Dartmoor Prison, two convicts called William Silvester and Fergus Frith made a well publicised escape from that institution. At about that same time, ACD was completing the 3rd instalment of *The Hound of the Baskervilles* (Chapters V-VI of XV) and introduced a character called Selden, a fugitive from 'the great convict prison of Princetown'.

On 17th June 1901, the proof of the 2nd instalment of *The Hound of the Baskervilles* (Chapters III-IV of XV) was returned to ACD and he informed the editor of *The Strand Magazine* that the 3rd instalment (Chapters V-VI of XV) was nearly finished. At the end of June 1901, ACD sent the

4th and 5th instalments (Chapters VII-IX of XV) to *The Strand Magazine*.

During mid-July 1901, ACD went on holiday to the Esplanade Hotel in Southsea, having recently submitted the 6th and 7th instalments of *The Hound of the Baskervilles* (Chapters X-XII of XV). Indeed, ACD sent corrections to *The Strand Magazine* from Southsea. During August 1901, the first of 9 monthly instalments of *The Hound of the Baskervilles* appeared in British editions of *The Strand Magazine* (see Plate 63). BFR's contribution was acknowledged in a brief footnote to Chapter I as follows:

> This story owes its inception to my friend, Mr. Fletcher Robinson, who has helped me both in the general plot and in the local details. — A.C.D.

In September 1901, the 1st of 9 monthly instalments of *The Hound of the Baskervilles* appeared in the American edition of *The Strand Magazine*. During this same month, ACD also completed writing the final two instalments (Chapters XIII-XV) at his home called Undershaw at Hindhead in Surrey. By this time the story had increased in length to some 60,000 words meaning that ACD was due to be paid £6,000 for the serialisation. It is interesting to note that entries in ACD's account book for 1901 reveal that he paid BFR over £500 before the end of that year.

Plate 63. Cover of the British edition of
The Strand Magazine (November 1901).

Plate 64. The first British book edition
(published 25th March 1902).

On 25th March 1902, *The Hound of the Baskervilles* was
published as a novel by George Newnes, London (see Plate
64). It preceded by 1 month the publication of the final

episode in the British edition of *The Strand Magazine*. The British book edition carries the following short acknowledgement on its own page that reads:

> *MY DEAR ROBINSON,*
>
> *It was to your account of a West-Country legend that this tale owes its inception. For this and for your help in the details all thanks.*
>
> *Yours most truly,*
>
> *A. CONAN DOYLE.*
>
> HINDHEAD,
> HASLEMERE.

Sometime thereafter, BFR gave 1st British edition copies of *The Hound of the Baskervilles* to The Revd Robert Duins Cooke, Agnes Cooke (wife of The Revd Cooke) and 'Harry' Baskerville. Each book contains the following handwritten inscription that purports to the extent of BFR's involvement with the story:

> *To Rev. R D Cooke from the assistant plot producer, Bertram Fletcher Robinson*
>
> *To Mrs. Cooke, with the kind regards of the assistant plot producer, Bertram Fletcher Robinson*
>
> *To Harry Baskerville from B Fletcher Robinson with apologies for using the name!*

BERTRAM FLETCHER ROBINSON

On 15th April 1902, *The Hound of the Baskervilles* was published as a novel by McClure, Phillips and Company (New York). This, the 1st American edition of the book, includes a version of ACD's acknowledgement letter to BFR. This version was written, from dictation, on 26th January 1902, by Major Charles Terry (ACD's secretary) and it therefore predates the acknowledgement published in the 1st British edition. This letter is now held by the Berg Collection in New York Public Library and reads:

MY DEAR ROBINSON

It was your account of a west country legend which first suggested the idea of this little tale to my mind. For this, and for the help which you gave me in its evolution, all thanks. Yours most truly, A. Conan Doyle.

The monthly sales of the British edition of *The Strand Magazine* doubled in circulation to nearly 300,000 copies during the serialisation of *The Hound of the Baskervilles*. The 1st British book edition sold nearly 25,000 copies prior to the publication of the final episode in that same magazine during April 1902. The 1st American book edition sold at the rate of 5,000 copies per day for the first 10 days after its publication. Moreover, this tale has since formed the basis for at least 19 full-length films in 6 different languages. Hence, it is the most filmed fictional story of all time.

Chapter 7

Dartmoor

During 1882, 11 year-old BFR moved from his school at Liscard near the city of Liverpool, to the rural village of Ipplepen. There can be little doubt that this was somewhat of a culture shock to him. Nevertheless, BFR quickly adapted to his new environment and soon developed an enduring interest for Dartmoor. The southern edge of this 369 square mile area of high moorland is located just 6 miles to the north of Ipplepen. Indeed, many of its granite hills (tors) are clearly visible from both Park Hill Cross and St. Andrew's Church. Between 1884 and 1890, BFR visited the area with various Newton College teams to play away fixtures. He also rode-to-hounds there, together with his father and other members of both the South Devonshire Hunt and Dart Vale Harriers. Finally, it appears that he frequently fished Dartmoor's rivers and streams with his best friend, Harold Michelmore.

During the 1880's there was an increased interest in the historical monuments of Dartmoor. Perhaps this shaped BFR's decision to study History at Jesus College (1890-1893)? In any event, the desire to record Dartmoor's threatened antiquities ultimately led The Devonshire Association to found a 6 member Dartmoor Exploration Committee (1894). The group secretary was the prolific author and local historian, The Revd Sabine Baring Gould. This committee undertook various projects including an 1894/95 excavation of 24 stone huts at the ancient Bronze-Age fortress of Grimspound. All findings were published in the annual *Report and Transactions of the Devonshire*

Association. BFR had access to that periodical through his father, who was a member of The Devonshire Association between 1884 and 1903. BFR also refers to that same organisation in his Dartmoor-based story entitled *The Mystery of Thomas Hearne* (1905).

Little is known about the 1901 trip that ACD and BFR undertook to Dartmoor in connection with *The Hound of the Baskervilles*. The only first-hand accounts of that trip are the letter that ACD wrote to his mother and the comments that are attributed to BFR by HJW Dam (see Chapter 6). These items suggest that on Saturday 1st June 1901, the pair departed Princetown and then walked 14 miles across Dartmoor on a route that encompassed Fox Tor Mires and Grimspound. The former location appears to be the inspiration for 'the great Grimpen Mire' and the latter, for the stone-hut that was inhabited by Sherlock Holmes. However, what else might BFR and ACD discussed and viewed during their hike across Dartmoor?

The answer to the foregoing question will never be known of course. However, the authors recently rediscovered the following article about Dartmoor that was written by BFR and published in *Pearson's Magazine* during September 1904. In this piece, BFR states that 'It is now many years since I first set eyes upon one of the stone villages of the moor, but the impression which those dwellings of prehistoric man produced is still with me.' He also makes a passing reference to legends of 'ghost packs that go screaming by in the night watches, of pixies and uncanny elves, of demons and fairies.' Such tantalizing comments are probably the closest that we will ever come to knowing what was actually discussed and seen by BFR and ACD during their research-trip to Dartmoor.

BERTRAM FLETCHER ROBINSON

Remains of the massive double wall which surrounds the ancient fortress of Grimspound on Dartmoor. It is 3000 years old at a moderate reckoning, and a colossal amount of time and labour must have been spent on it by its primitive builders.

HISTORIC MONUMENTS OF BRITAIN.

The Ancient Britons of the Stone Age, the Romans who conquered Briton at the commencement of the Christian era, the Saxons, Normans and Danes, who have played their part in the making of Britain and Britain's history, have all left behind them indestructible traces of their lives, and the influence they exerted in the land. These traces consist of such venerable monuments of history as the "Druid" relics at Stonehenge, the ancient fortress of Grimspound, on Dartmoor, the Roman Wall and the many other Roman remains; no more interesting expedition could be thought of than a visit to these historic spots. And whether a visit be possible or not, we feel sure that readers of "Pearson's Magazine" will read with interest authoritative accounts of these places, as they were and as they are. The Roman City of Silchester (near Reading) and the Roman Wall from Newcastle to Carlisle have already been dealt with. Next month a vivid pen picture will be painted of Roman Chester.

III.—THE FORTRESS OF THE FIRST BRITONS.

A Description of the Fortress of Grimspound, on Dartmoor.

By B. FLETCHER ROBINSON.

IT was not until recent years that people living beyond its boundaries had any intimacy with the wild, mysterious region known as Dartmoor. Yet there is no place in the British Isles better deserving of attention. The "forest," as the old documents term it, bears no resemblance to the Scottish moors, nor the melancholy wastes of Ireland.

An indented rampart of hills encircles it, a frowning barrier that bars the vast tableland behind it from the smiling cultivation that stretches at its feet. Sunny cornfields, broad woods, rosy orchards spread out in gentle undulations, while above them hangs the moor, a sinister, storm-swept land of desolation, patched with mires that will drag down horse and man, bare of bush and tree, its rolling surface crowned with gigantic outcrops like the ruins of a thousand feudal castles. It is this strong contrast

108

BERTRAM FLETCHER ROBINSON

The gateway of Grimspound as it remains to-day. The huge granite blocks that it is made up of are unwieldy and of colossal weight and size, yet with no labour-saving implements of any sort the Ancient British tribesmen quarried them and placed them in position

that renders Dartmoor itself so memorable and surprising.

Century has followed century, and left the moor unchanged save for a field or two won from the mires and stone-scattered wastes of ling. The population is decreasing year by year; cottages in the scattered hamlets fall into ruinous decay. But it is from the stubborn face which the moor has turned to the men who would try to fence and drain and cultivate it that it is now the chosen spot for the study of our far-away ancestors who lived in England before the Saxons, before the Romans, even before the ancient British, as we call the Celtic tribes whom Cæsar's legions fought and conquered. Undisturbed in the heart of the solitary wilderness stand their huts and walls, their stone avenues and monuments, their circles and kistevens, very much as their builders left them three thousand years ago.

These builders—whence were they? No one can say with any certainty. They were dwelling on the land when the advance guard of the Celtic invasion—the Ancient Britons of the history books—came over the North Sea. They knew no metal, flint taking its place as hammer and axe-head, as scraper and chisel;

yet they had sufficient mechanical knowledge to rear great rocks on end, to build huge walls, and plant long avenues of stone.

Neolithic men the scientists call them; narrow-headed, dark and agile folk, with great knowledge of Nature and her laws. It was the bronze man who defeated them with his heavy cutting weapons, which were to the flint as a Lee-Metford to a Brown Bess.

It is now many years since I first set eyes upon one of the stone villages of the moor, but the impression which those dwellings of prehistoric man produced is still with me.

I had walked from Brent on Dartmoor's southern edge, northward up the desolate valley of the Avon. By Black Tor I went, and on over Ryders Plain till I climbed the ridge beyond Huntingdon Warren. It was a gloomy day. Sheets of mist were gathering on the upper moor where lay the infamous marshes of Awne and Fox Tor, vast bogs that take their toll of cattle yearly and hold many a wayfarer's bones in their black depths. The great shoulder of Holne hunched itself on the eastern skyline. Not a sign of modern habitation marked the existence of man.

109

BERTRAM FLETCHER ROBINSON

The gateway of Grimspound as it appeared in the days when the wonderful fortress was first built. The fortress was used as a refuge for the herds and flocks of the tribe in time of danger, and the entrance was paved with granite in order that they should not trample it into a morass.

Suddenly on a distant slope I caught sight of a grey circle of tumbled stone, upon the brown hillside. As I advanced, another and another sprang into view. I pulled out a field-glass and the lens showed me that here was no freak of nature, but the ruins of a village, or rather of many villages. I could trace the space allotted to each hut with perfect ease.

Who could they have been, these dwellers in the wilderness ? They must have numbered several thousands, have built their dwellings according to the orders of their chief, have banded together for defence and lived remote lives as herdsmen on the moor. It was from that date that I commenced to make inquiries into the evidence of habits and customs that these earliest of west country men have left to us in hut and monument and implement.

Perhaps the most remarkable of the remains upon Dartmoor is the fortified refuge camp of Grimspound. Its vast walls and circular dwellings, though ruined, remain to prove its original design. As to the life of those who lived therein, no man can write without treading on the toes of some learned authority. Yet, despite the fact that some theorist may cry out at the neglect of his assertions, the main facts are sufficiently plain.

In the lonely heart of the moor, set in a shallow valley to the left of the road from Chagford to Two Bridges, lies the stronghold of Grimspound. If you stand upon Hooknor Tor, above this broad indentation, the circle of defensive wall spreads before you like a gigantic mushroom ring, the grey stones showing clearly against the sombre hues of the stunted heather.

It is not until you reach the entrance, however, that you realise the labour that its building must have entailed upon tribes whose only tools were of flint, and whose means of heavy transport were rough sledges dragged by the united strength of hundreds.

The interior, some four acres in extent, was surrounded by two walls which, by the storms of centuries, have been thrown down and mingled into a low broad mound of granite boulders.

Some of these rocks are enormous. On the west side is a huge slab 10ft. by 5ft., from 9in. to 1ft. in thickness, and weighing from

BERTRAM FLETCHER ROBINSON

three to four tons. There are many other stones laid in regular courses that are of equal weight. Such a fortification at the present day with every labour-saving device of the modern contractor would cost at least £3 10s. a yard, each yard requiring the work of four men for a week! And Grimspound had an inner and outer wall, one a little less and one a little more than five hundred yards in circumference!

The garrison—for the huts are so few that they were undoubtedly intended for a garrison and not for peaceful herdsmen—are twenty-four in number. The central hut, which probably belonged to the chief, is in excellent repair; it is circular, and the interior is close upon 11ft. across. The entrance was by a curved passage through which the incomer passed on hands and knees, but, once inside, matters improved. The granite walls were 3ft. 9in. in height, and from them sprang the wooden beams which supported a roof, something after the style of a bell tent. Doubtless the roof was of reed thatch, with a hole at the top for a chimney.

Across one side there runs a daïs, or platform of stone, some eight inches in height, upon which the chief reclined by day and slept at night. A hearth, a deep cook-hole set with stones, an anvil for splitting bones—such is the interior as time has left it; and there is no reason to believe that its inhabitants suffered great misery or privation. Across the door a skin curtain would turn the blasts which might eddy down the curving passage. Turf and banks of soil outside the walls would keep them wind and rain proof.

Within the huts the floor was paved and dry; the fire crackled on the hearth, the red-hot cooking stones, many of which remain, roasted the meat in the cook-hole. My lord and his wife, or wives, tired by a long day in the vigorous air, devoured their supper with

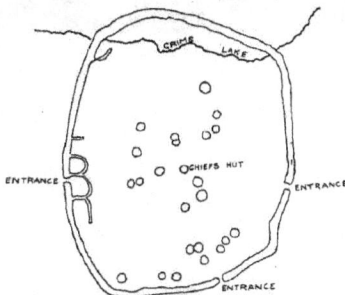

A map of Grimspound, reconstructed from the remains that can be seen to-day on Dartmoor. In its prosperous days the huts were probably far more numerous than is shown here.

gusto in the splendid isolation of the daïs, while the servants waited on them.

They drank from skins, like the men of the desert do to-day; they and their cattle were safe enough from man or beast behind such mighty ramparts. It was no palace of the Pharaohs, no golden hall of Babylon; but these neolithic gentlemen did not repine for luxuries of which they had never heard. Instead, they slept the sleep of the just till dawn came stealing up from behind the Hey Tor range to the eastward, and thanked their gods that in so uncertain a world another day of life remained to them.

From the charcoal buried by the fireplaces and the logs cut from the peat, from the flint arrow-heads and implements, from the position of the fortress and the huts that cluster into unprotected villages in its neighbourhood, we can, without undue guesswork, build up a picture of the famous stronghold of Grimspound as in the height of its fame it frowned across the moor three thousand years ago.

The eternal wastes were the same then as now, save that in the valleys below the fortress were copses of trees and thickets of scrub oak and hazel. Over the edge of the moor, however, in the lowlands beyond the rampart of the sentinel tors, flourished vast forests of such primeval density that to clear them for human settlement involved immense labour; while with bear and wolf and fox lurking in the thickets around, the pasturage of the herds was attended by daily loss. It was for this reason that the little dark-haired men had sought the upper ground, preferring its storms and hurricanes to the hidden dangers in a warmer, less exposed country. They were plucky fellows, clad in skins, with bows in their hands and flint-topped arrows at their waists. Upon the open tracts around them they could feed and guard their herds.

111

BERTRAM FLETCHER ROBINSON

A distant view from an overlooking hill of the fortress of Grimspound; the circle of the double wall—now more than half demolished by the elements—can be distinctly traced, besides the ruins of many of the huts.

The tribes increased and prospered. The little round huts grew more numerous. Great men arose and died amongst them, receiving honour in their death by laborious monuments of stone. At last the ravages of the wolves that thinned the herds and flocks in winter became too expensive to be borne. Also, there were wars, tribe fighting against tribe with arrow, club, and flint hatchet. So in the end, all the men whose villages lay scattered about Hambledon moors, and King Tor, and Shapeley Common united in building a central fortress of defence which we know as Grimspound.

The other tribes followed their example in the deeper fastnesses of the moor, but their efforts were far less gigantic. Perhaps it was that Grimspound lay nearer the southern edge of the table land, and that strangers, spying out the country from the southward, met its garrison more often in war; perhaps, indeed, the other tribes lent their aid in raising this fortress to guard the southern trackways.

The permanent garrison was small, not perhaps more than two hundred all told. Probably the chief who lived there made them his guard of retainers. The central hut was his palace. On the wide spreading

stretches of moorland his subjects were scattered in their villages. The hardy cattle and flocks of tiny short-haired sheep pastured on the slopes. In the more sheltered valleys patches of some rough kind of grain were grown.

There remain, indeed, traces of long ledges carved in the west and south slopes that suggest such terraces as you may see to-day in the hill borders of India, terraces carved and cultivated by the natives. They had amongst them cunning hunters, and many a wild stag or humble rabbit would find its way to the tribal larders.

It is not difficult to picture an alarm of war. The horns would echo over the moors, sending the women and children scurrying for shelter to the Grimspound gates. Household goods were scanty in those days, and the stock of skins and flint tools, of bone needles and hide thread could easily be carried by the non-combatants, while the fathers and brothers rounded up the cattle and drove them within the great walls.

The gateways were paved so that the hoofs of the herds should not churn them into deep morasses of mud.

When all were in safety and the wooden gates closed, the enemy could be set at

112

BERTRAM FLETCHER ROBINSON

The remains of the chief's hut that stood—and stands—in the centre of the fortress of Grimspound. It is, circumstances considered, in a remarkable state of preservation, and has now been railed in to protect it from the ravages of man and beast.

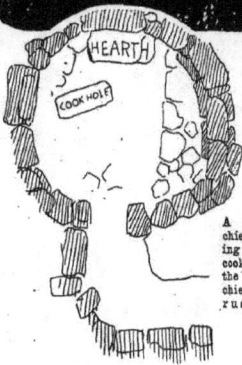

A plan of the chief's hut, showing the hearth, cook-hole, and, on the right, the chief's couch — a rude affair of stone.

defiance. According to modern ideas, it would be difficult to imagine a more weakly-situated place of defence; the tors to right and left closely overhang the fortress, and a Plantagenet archer could have picked off the garrison at his leisure; but in those times, when bows were small and the clumsy flint-tipped arrows had no great penetration, there was little danger in a long-range bombardment.

The low-lying position had undoubtedly been chosen for its regular supply of water; a stream entered beneath the wall and passed through the interior space for some thirty yards before making its exit. On the heights above there would have been no water for the

besieged or their cattle; moreover, in so exposed a place they would have suffered the full fury of the storms, with resultant heavy loss amongst the flocks and herds during the winter months.

Yet careful measurement proves that there were places on the upper slopes where the most primitive arrow and sling fire could not have failed to inflict loss on the garrison as they moved about the interior, or to gall the penned-up beasts to frenzy. This possible danger had also been provided for by the cunning neolithic tribe.

The encircling wall was, as I have said, double. Sufficient traces remain amongst the tumbled granite blocks to prove that fact without a doubt. In the alley-way between, the fighting men could run in safety without the danger of an arrow in their backs or a sling stone knocking in the base of their thick skulls.

The outer wall was three feet thick at the bottom and about six feet high. Along the crest of the wall, however, it seems plain that mud and turf was banked, just as the Devon farmers bank them to-day, so that the total height was from eight to nine feet. The

113

BERTRAM FLETCHER ROBINSON

inner wall, which was some five feet in height, would offer ample protection to the backs of men who did not themselves exceed that stature.

Against the inner wall are the remains of stone pens or folds. Here the cattle would be gathered under the cover of the fortifications. Where the pens were commanded from the outer slopes additional side walls would protect the beasts; there may also have been shields of hide stretched on wooden frames as a further defence from long-distance arrow fire.

with many-coloured sails and bore away the metal to the sunny lands of the East.

The monuments to the dead and the sacred circles on Dartmoor are amongst the most remarkable of neolithic mysteries. It is no matter for surprise that strange rumours concerning them should have grown amongst the solitary moormen, and that we should hear of ghost packs that go screaming by in the night watches, of pixies and uncanny elves, of demons and fairies.

The great menhir in lonely Drizzlecombe is a narrow pillar tapering from four feet

The chief's hut in Grimspound as it must have appeared when built. It was probably thatched in some way with turf or peat, and had at the top a hole to let out the smoke. Probably in windy weather a curtain made of hide was hung inside the entrance.

Such were the defences of Grimspound. As the centuries rolled by, it may be that, after battle and massacre, Grimspound was inhabited by the Celtic invaders, the ancient Britons, who in turn yielded to Cæsar and his Roman legions. Across the valley the hills are scarped and torn by those who mined for tin in the most primitive of fashions. It may be that Grimspound, grown older, was a very Birmingham of the moors, sending its loads of tin on pony-back down to Totnes upon the River Dart, where the swarthy-faced Phœnicians brought their ship

thick at the base to two and a half at the summit. Eighteen feet in height it stands with a weight of seven tons. Near Newlycombe Lake a chieftain's grave stands in a circle of stones, from which stretches a line of upright rocks, one hundred and seventy-three in number, occupying six hundred yards in length. The biggest stone weighs over three tons, and stands nine feet in height. Beneath that wild mountain, Great Mistor, in a stoneless waste of moor rises a circle of upright rocks, each six to seven feet long. For what purpose were they laboriously built?

114

BERTRAM FLETCHER ROBINSON

It is plain that these neolithic men had great respect for the dead—a respect as great as that in which the Chinese or the South Sea Islanders hold their ancestors. Almost undoubtedly it was to the dead chieftains that these mighty monuments were raised.

Their labours must have been extraordinary. Though the whole tribe toiled together, weeks and months must have gone by before the great works were completed.

It is hardly possible to understand how the flint hammer and bone chisel carved the granite block into a shape however rough and irregular. Yet these things were done and stand now, a cause for admiration and wonder to the twentieth century.

The difficulties in the way of those who would see for themselves these relics of an age that is gone are considerable. But the fact that railways—save for the single line that winds up the wooded valley from Plymouth until it emerges upon the wastes to find its terminus at Princetown—have left Dartmoor

an unviolated sanctuary of the few remaining monuments of the first of all the Britons must carry with it a certain sense of satisfaction; and though the trouble in reaching Grimspound is by that fact made proportionately greater, compensation is found in the old-world atmosphere that still clings around the ruins, that seem destined to be free from the attentions of modern vandals.

The best ways of reaching Grimspound are from Princetown and from Moreton Hampstead—the latter on a Great Western branch line. The first is distant about nine miles from the ruins; the latter about six.

A map of the moor will show the circles and avenues, the forts and monuments; but let the traveller beware, for bogs are deep, and sudden mists most numerous. For walks into the interior of the wilderness it is well to choose a clear, hard day, or to take a guide. But possible hardships and difficulties notwithstanding, he who penetrates into the wilds of Dartmoor is well repaid for his trouble.

Photo by Valentine.
A stone avenue near Castor on Dartmoor. It was probably erected by neolithic Britons as a monument to a dead chieftain.

115

Chapter 8

Post-Hound London

On 22nd April 1902, just 1 week after the publication of the first American book edition of *The Hound of the Baskervilles*, the Victorian artist, 68 year-old Philip Richard Morris (see Plate 65) died of 'bladder disease (3 years) and heart failure (2 days)'. He was the widowed father of BFR's fiancé, Gladys Hill Morris and an Associate of the Royal Academy of Arts (elected 18th June 1877). Philip Morris was born on 4th December 1833 at Devonport in Devon and was admitted as a student to the Royal Academy on 25th April 1854. Philip Morris is perhaps best remembered for his oil painting entitled *Son's of the Brave* that was first exhibited during 1880.

Plate 65. Philip Richard Morris (1892).
© NATIONAL PORTRAIT GALLERY. ALL RIGHTS RESERVED (x7381)

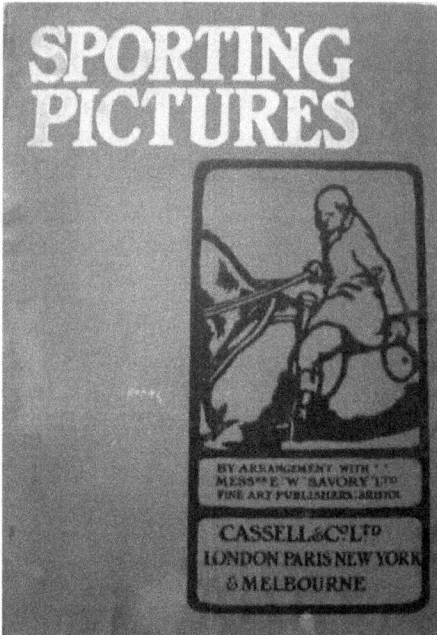

Plate 66. *Sporting Pictures* (1902).

On 23rd April 1902, Cassell & Company published a book entitled *Sporting Pictures* (see Plate 66). It features 36 reproductions of paintings on outdoor sports by various artists. BFR wrote some 25,000 words of 'descriptive letterpress' to accompany the large chromolithographs that were prepared by E.W. Savory Limited of Park Row Studios in Bristol (Savory also acted as editor). The interconnecting narrative reveals that BFR had a thorough knowledge of many sports, including cricket, hockey, rugby football, riding to hounds, stag hunting, angling, shooting, golf, rowing and horse racing. This is now a scarce volume because print dealers frequently removed the plates and resold them as individually framed items.

BERTRAM FLETCHER ROBINSON

On 3rd June 1902, 31 year-old BFR married a 22 year-old self-proclaimed 'actress' called Gladys Hill Morris at St. Barnabas Church, Kensington, London. The marriage was witnessed by BFR's parents, Percy Illingworth and 'Bowden' (see Chapter 2). BFR recorded his address at that time as 4 Addison Crescent, the home of his uncle, Sir John Robinson. Thereafter, the newly-weds resided at nearby 43 Buckingham Palace Mansions. This property was built around 1894 and the previous occupier was a Miss Fane, who in turn had acquired the property from one Percival Wolton. It is worth noting that ACD used 15 Buckingham Palace Mansions as his town rooms from about 1923. The property has since been demolished.

On 15th July 1902, 19 year-old John Philip Claude Morris (BFR's brother-in-law) joined the Royal Navy as an 'Assistant Clerk' and was posted to the flagship battleship *HMS Bulwark* in the Mediterranean (commanded by Admiral Sir Compton Domvile). It is possible that this decision was prompted by the recent death of Philip Morris, who appears to have died in straightened circumstances and left no Last Will and Testament. Service records reveal that 'Claude' was later promoted to the rank of 'Clerk' (*HMS Venus*; 15th July 1903), 'Assistant Paymaster' (*HMS Venus*; 26th October 1905), 'Assistant Paymaster & Captain's Clerk' (*HMS Excellent*; 16th July 1907) and 'Secretary to the Personal Staff' of Rear-Admiral Reginald Tupper (*HMS Prince of Wales*; 18th November 1912). He also served as 'Secretary to the Personal Staff' of Rear Admiral Sydney Fremantle (*HMS Hibernia*, 27th July 1915). It should be noted that Claude registered BFR's death during 1907 (see Chapter 9).

BERTRAM FLETCHER ROBINSON

During December 1902, *The Windsor Magazine* began the publication of 6 episodes of a monthly serial adventure that was written by BFR and John Malcolm Fraser and collectively entitled *The Trail Of The Dead – The Strange Experience Of Dr. Robert Harland* (edited by A. Hutchinson). This periodical was published by Ward Lock & Company Limited of London and was the most successful rival at that time to *The Strand Magazine*. The 6 episodes are entitled as follows: *I. The Hairy Caterpillar, II. The Mystery Of The Lemsdorf Ham, III. The Chase In The Snow, IV. The Anonymous Article, V. The Ammonia Cylinder, VI. The End Of The Trail.* These tales feature an insane Professor who leaves a trail of murdered colleagues strewn across Europe. Each episode appears to be set in a location that BFR had visited whilst he was researching *Capitals at Play* for *Cassell's Magazine* (1897). Fraser worked with BFR as 'Day Editor' of the *Daily Express* between 1902 and 1904. Later, Fraser was knighted (1919), created a baronet (1921) and awarded the Knight Grand Cross of the Order of the British Empire (1922).

On 6th February 1903, Geraldine Winn Everett was born at Oaklands, 276 Barnet Lane, Elstree, Hertfordshire. She was the daughter of BFR's friend and colleague Percy Everett, the then 'Literary Editor' of the *Daily Express* (see Plate 67). Later, he held the editorship of Pearson's *The Novel Magazine* and was knighted in 1930 for his work with the Boy Scouts and Girl Guides Association. BFR, never fathered a child of his own, but he acted as godfather to baby 'Winn'. She later worked as a physician at Elstree in Hertfordshire. Coincidentally, Winn died on 21st January 1998, on the 91st anniversary of BFR's death.

Plate 67. Sir Percy Everett (left)
COURTESY OF THE TOPFOTO COLLECTION

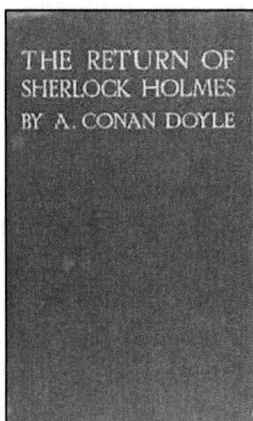

Plate 68. *The Return of Sherlock Holmes* (1905).

During May 1903, *Pearson's Magazine* published a BFR short story entitled *The Battle of Fingle's Bridge* (Vol. XV, pp. 530-536). This is a fairy tale, told by a small boy who falls asleep upon a moor and witnesses a battle between the 'people of the ferns and rushes' and the 'people of the gorse and heather'. All the characters are 6 inches tall and are dressed in medieval garb and armour and have miniature horses and weapons. The boy, aided by a fairy, becomes involved in the battle and finally awakens to find signs of the battle on the moor. There is a Fingle Bridge, over the River Teign, which is a famous tourist beauty spot near Drewsteignton, on the north-eastern border of Dartmoor. It is interesting to note that on 24th February 1923, *The Western Morning News and Mercury* printed an interview with ACD in which, he is quoted as stating a belief in Devonshire fairies.

During July 1903, BFR's father, 76 year-old Joseph Fletcher Robinson, underwent an operation in London. On 8th August of that same year, he returned to Park Hill House in Ipplepen where he died just 3 days later. Joseph was buried nearby at St. Andrew's Church beside his friend, The Revd Douglas Stewart. The funeral service was conducted by The Revd Robert Duins Cooke who had accompanied BFR on a research trip to Dartmoor in connection with *The Hound of the Baskervilles*.

On 22nd August 1903, the *Mid-Devon and Newton Times* reported that Joseph Fletcher Robinson's funeral was attended by Mrs. Emily Robinson (wife), Mr. and Mrs. B. Fletcher Robinson, Sir John Robinson, Mrs. Holt (BFR's maternal Aunt) and Harold Michelmore. Thereafter, Joseph's estate was proved at £16,218 11s 0d net and Sidney Hacker was granted probate. He was a senior partner in a Newton Abbot based firm of solicitors called

Hacker, Michelmore and Wilkinson. Emily was named as the principal beneficiary to the estate and she used part of her inheritance to install a commemorative stained-glass window in the south-side of the Chancel of St. Andrew's Church. It depicts the figures of Our Lady and Child, with St. John the Divine and St. Andrew and was designed by the noted Victorian artist, Charles Eamer Kempe. Kempe also designed windows for York Minster Cathedral.

During September 1903, BFR and Illingworth were each admitted as founder members of the Jesus College Cambridge Society (JCCS). The JCCS was co-founded by Dr. Henry Menzies who studied at Jesus College between 1886 and 1894 (he was affectionately referred to as 'Blucher'). Between 1897 and 1918, Menzies ran a private practice from his home at 4 Ashley Gardens, just 50 meters from where Lewis, Illingworth and BFR had resided at 126 Ashley Gardens. Menzies was the first 'Secretary' to 'The Society' and was later elected 'Life-Honorary Secretary'. Between 1904 and 1907, the JCCS *Annual Report* listed Menzies, BFR and Illingworth as members. It is interesting to note that Menzies was the physician who certified BFR's death during 1907 (see Chapter 9).

On 31st October 1903, ACD had a Sherlock Holmes story entitled *The Adventure of the Norwood Builder* published in *Collier's Weekly Magazine*. It was the 2nd episode in a series of 13 short stories that was written for that same periodical following the success of *The Hound of the Baskervilles*. In this story, an innocent person is incriminated for a murder by the use of a wax mould to falsify their thumbprint. Harold Michelmore reported that ACD bought this idea from BFR during a voyage aboard the *S.S. Briton* in July 1900 (see Chapter 5). Hence, BFR made contributions to the plots of 2 of the first 3 stories that were written after the apparent death of Sherlock Holmes at the Reichenbach Falls during December 1893. On 7th March 1905, George Newnes compiled and republished all 13 short stories in a book entitled *The Return of Sherlock Holmes* (see Plate 68). *The Adventure of the Norwood Builder* was followed by a further 30 Sherlock Holmes tales (December 1903 - February 1927).

On 21st November 1903, 70 year-old Sir Charles Seale-Hayne was 'seized with apoplexy' and died the following day aged 70 years (see Chapter 2). BFR was subsequently short-listed as the prospective Liberal Parliamentary Candidate for the Mid or Ashburton Division of Devonshire. However, this candidacy was eventually awarded to a local farmer called Harry Trelawny Eve. On 8th January 1904, Eve defeated the Unionist Parliamentary Candidate (Conservative), General Sir Richard Harrison, in a by-election. It is perhaps worth noting that 2 years later, BFR's friends, Lehmann, Illingworth and ACD each contested a parliamentary seat for the Liberal Party (elected, elected and defeated respectively).

On 30th November 1903, 75 year-old Sir John Robinson died at 4 Addison Crescent from 'cardiac failure and congestion of the lungs (4 days)'. Earlier that same day he is reported as having remarked to his staff 'I do not feel the desire to converse – kindly respect my wishes.' Sir John bequeathed £500 to Frederick Robinson, his only surviving brother. He also gave £100 to the widow of his friend and former employee, Frederick Moy Thomas. Thomas helped Sir John to produce an autobiography by compiling his vast collection of personal papers. He also wrote the preface, in which, he acknowledged the assistance that was given to him by members of Sir John's family. It is very probable that these unnamed individuals included BFR who had resided with Sir John at 4 Addison Crescent (1901-1902) and also had extensive editorial experience.

During December 1903, a group of 6 men founded an 'invited member only' criminology club in London. 'Our Society' or the 'Crimes Club' would meet for dinner and to hear a paper that was both prepared and read by one of the members. These events were intended to be 'strictly private' and so were usually conducted at a member's home. The original founders included the author and journalist, Arthur Lambton, the physician and barrister, Samuel Ingleby Oddie and the qualified barrister and actor 'Harry Brodribb Irving (eldest son of the actor, Sir Henry Irving). Shortly thereafter, a further 6 members were admitted to the society and these included BFR, ACD and Max Pemberton.

During February 1904, *The Trail of the Dead* by BFR and J. Malcolm Fraser was published as a single volume by Ward, Lock & Company Limited of London. That same year, it was also published by Langton Hall of Toronto in Canada. The British and Canadian book editions were released in hardcover and paperback formats respectively (see Plate 69). Both editions number 215 pages and feature 16 illustrations by the artist, Adolf Thiede. Moreover, they each contain 6 chapters that correspond to the order of episodes as serialized by *The Windsor Magazine* (December 1902 - May 1903). It is interesting to note that both book editions carry only BFR's name on the front-cover and spine. This might suggest that he was the senior contributor to this collaboration.

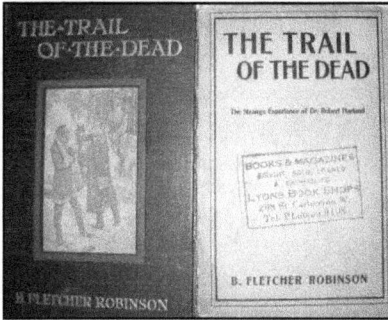

Plate 69. The British and Canadian book editions of *The Trail of the Dead* (left & right respectively).

During May 1904, BFR replaced Oliver Fry as the 'Editor' of a periodical entitled *Vanity Fair*. Shortly thereafter, BFR switched publishing companies from Arthur Evans to Alfred Harmsworth (Lord Northcliffe). During his editorship, BFR bylined many of the leader articles and there are indications that he wrote others under various pseudonyms. *Vanity Fair* is perhaps best remembered for publishing caricatures of famous people (see Plate 70) that were drawn by artists such as 'Ape' (Carlo Pellegrini, 1838-1889) and most famously, 'Spy' (Leslie Ward, 1851-1922). Each cartoon was accompanied by a short and a highly entertaining biography. The original proprietor and editor of *Vanity Fair* was Thomas Bowles (1841-1922) who supposedly wrote 2,300 biographies under the pseudonym of 'Jehu Junior' during the 5 decades of the magazine's existence (1868-1914). However, this is improbable because Bowles sold the magazine during 1889. It is therefore more likely, that the pseudonym 'Jehu Junior' was a hereditary title that passed between editors. In any event, the first BFR bylined item to appear in *Vanity Fair* was published on 26th May 1904 and entitled, *Women of Civilisation*.

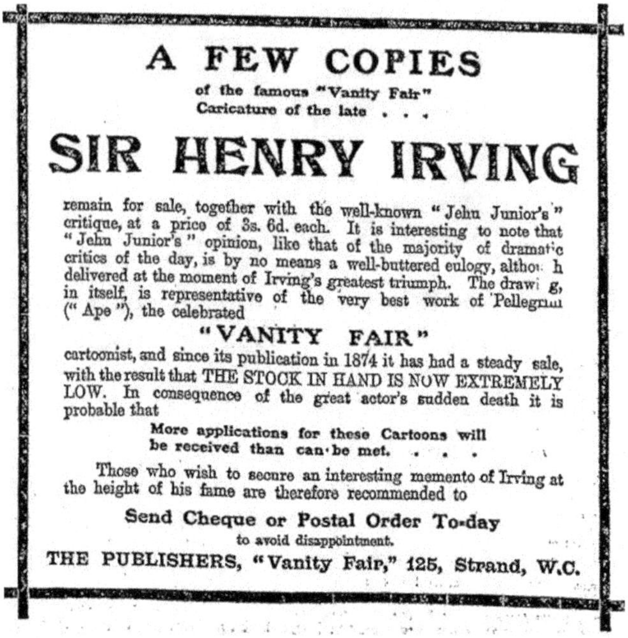

Plate 70. An advertisement for *Vanity Fair* that appeared in *The Times* newspaper (17th October 1905)

On 18th June 1904, both BFR and ACD attended a dinner at the Savoy Hotel in London that was held to honour Lord Roberts. This dinner was hosted by Joseph Hodges Choate, the then American Ambassador to the United Kingdom (1899-1905). The guest list included many British dignitaries, all of whom were members of an Anglo-American society entitled 'The Pilgrims'. This organisation was founded during 1902 in order 'to promote good-will, good-fellowship, and everlasting peace between the United States and Great Britain'. Over the years it has boasted an elite membership of politicians, diplomats, businessmen, and writers. The Pilgrims still convene to welcome into office each successive US Ambassador to the UK and each new UK Ambassador to the US. The current patron of the society is Her Majesty Queen Elizabeth II.

On 23rd June 1904, ACD had an item entitled *M.C.C. Absolutism* published under *Letters to the Editor* in *Vanity Fair*. ACD was himself a keen cricketer and member of the Marlyebone Cricket Club. This letter begins 'Sir,—You were good enough to ask me for my opinion of the management of the M.C.C.'. Evidently, BFR had relied upon his friendship with ACD to persuade the latter to write upon the topic.

On 7th July 1904, BFR had an article entitled *On Political Lies – A Growing Danger in British Politics*, published in *Vanity Fair*. In this article, BFR accused politicians from both the Liberal and Labour parties of using misinformation to promote their causes. He cites lies being told about the 2nd Boer War, exaggerations about rising food prices and the falsification of data pertaining to the number of Chinese immigrants working the mines. He exemplified the situation with a case involving his friend, ACD:

> In the last General Election [1900], Sir Arthur Conan Doyle was standing for a division of Edinburgh. The honesty of his convictions and his hard hitting, straight-forward oratory won him the hearts even

of political opponents. He had made great progress in the centre of a Radical stronghold, and his election seemed certain. On the day of the poll, however, the constituency was placarded with posters, stating in four-feet letters that Conan Doyle was a Roman Catholic, and that the Church of Scotland was in danger.

This Radical lie – for Sir Arthur does not happen to be a Roman catholic – caused the desired consternation. The worthy Scotsmen read, exclaimed in horror, and hurried to the polls to avert this terrible danger. An honourable method of winning an election surely!

BFR's reference to the integrity of ACD is particularly relevant given that it was written more than two years after the publication of *The Hound of the Baskervilles.* Evidently, BFR still held ACD in high esteem and was satisfied with the outcome of their literary collaboration during 1901. It is also interesting to note BFR's reference to the mine workers in South Africa. Both ACD and the fictional character of Sir Charles Baskerville in *The Hound of the Baskervilles*, had speculated in South African gold.

During August 1904, BFR had the first in a series of 6 detective short-stories collectively entitled *The Chronicles of Addington Peace*, published in Pearson's *The Lady's Home Magazine* (renamed *Home Magazine of Fiction* from November 1904). These separate stories are entitled as follows: *I. The Terror in the Snow, II. Mr. Taubery's*

Diamond, III. The Mystery of the Causeway, IV. The Vanished Millionaire, V. Mr. Coran's Election, VI. The Mystery of the Jade Spear. Each tale features Detective Inspector Addington Peace, 'a tiny slip of a fellow, of about five and thirty years of age.' Peace works for Scotland Yard's Criminal Investigation Department and is 'Watsoned' by an artist and neighbour called James Phillips. The 1st story in the serialisation was by-lined as follows: 'Joint author with Sir Arthur Conan Doyle in his Best Sherlock Holmes Story The Hound of the Baskervilles.' There is no indication that ACD objected to this statement. Hence, it appears that he was content to allow his name to be associated with BFR's work (see 1906).

On 11th August 1904, BFR had an article entitled *Pity Poor Agriculture! – Mr. Chamberlain's Facts, Suggestions, and Prophesies*, published in *Vanity Fair*. This article is a favourable review of Joseph Chamberlain's proposals for dealing with the agricultural depression then being experienced in Britain. Emphasis is given by BFR to Chamberlain's proposals on Tariff Reform that sought to protect British industry by banning the import of goods from outside the Empire. Readers will recall that in *The Hound of the Baskervilles*, the character of Sir Henry Baskerville is sent a note that warns him to 'keep away from the moor'. This anonymous message is largely derived from printed words that had been extracted from an imaginary leader about 'Free Trade' and Tariff Reform in *The Times* newspaper.

On 22nd November 1904, *The Times* newspaper announced the publication of Sir John Robinson's autobiography entitled *Fifty Years on Fleet Street* (London: McMillan & Company Limited). This book includes the following statement that is made in a foreword, which was written by Frederick Moy Thomas, a former employee of Sir John's for more than 25 years:

> I am much indebted to Sir Arthur Conan Doyle for leave to publish his striking letter to Sir John Robinson on the subject of America and the Americans [dated 3rd November 1894]…and to a number of Sir John's relatives and friends for similar facilities or for valuable counsel or assistance.

Clearly, ACD had granted permission for his letter to be reproduced in Sir John's autobiography. This further implies that ACD and the Robinson family were still on friendly terms some 3 years after the publication of *The Hound of the Baskervilles*.

Plate 71. PG Wodehouse

Plate 72. *The Chronicles of Addington Peace* (1905).
©BRITISH LIBRARY BOARD. ALL RIGHTS RESERVED (012632.cc15)

On 8th December 1904, BFR and Pelham Grenville Wodehouse (see Plate 71) had a playlet entitled *Our Christmas Pantomime – Little Red Riding Hood; or, The Virtuous British public and the Smart Set Wolf*, published in *Vanity Fair*. It is a satirical Christmas pantomime that features a mix of both literary and real characters. The pair co-authored a further 3 items prior to BFR's death during 1907. Wodehouse is perhaps best remembered for his series of short stories and novels that feature the characters of Bertie Wooster and Reginald Jeeves. He was made a Knight Commander of the Order of the British Order just 6 weeks before his death on 14th February 1975.

During June 1905, BFR had 8 short detective stories published in a book entitled *The Chronicles of Addington Peace* (Harper & Brother, London). This book (see Plate 72) features all 6 episodes from the *Lady's Home Magazine* plus 2 additional stories. These new stories are entitled *The Story of Amaroff the Pole* (Chapter I) and *The Mystery of Thomas Hearne* (Chapter V). The former story introduces Peace and Phillips within their home environment. The latter story resonates to some extent with *The Hound of the Baskervilles* in that it features an escaped convict on Dartmoor. This book is listed in the influential *Queens Quorum: A History of the Detective-Crime Short Story as Revealed by the 106 Most Important Books Published in this Field Since 1845*. In July 1998, both *The Chronicles of Addington Peace* and *The Trail of the Dead* were republished in a single volume by The Battered Silicon Dispatch Box of Ontario.

On 27th July 1905, BFR had a short story entitled *The Valley of Peace – Which May or May Not Be an Allegory*, published in *Vanity Fair*. This sentimental story appears to be set upon Dartmoor because the 'Valley of Peace' is described as 'being hidden on moorland which is occupied by hunting ghost hounds and covered by ramparts of hills and swamps which can swallow horses'. The story involves a father who promises his very young son that he will, when the son is old enough, take him to a secret valley on the moor. When the boy grows older, his father repeatedly finds excuses for not going there and eventually he dies. When the son himself is dying, he tells a companion that he is, at last, going to find the Valley of Peace, and expresses regret that he never visited it with his father.

On 17th August 1905, BFR had the first in a series of 5 semi-autobiographical short stories collectively entitled *The Chronicles of Pen* published by *Vanity Fair*. These separate tales each feature people that BFR had known as a boy when he lived in Ipplepen and are entitled as follows: *I. The Tact of Anne, II. The Unchivalric Conduct of M. Paul, III. - The Return of Gilbert Hare, IV. The Curious Coincidence of the Three Sermons, V. Mr. Mathers, Sportsman.* In the final story, BFR fondly recalls the times that he spent hunting during his school holidays (1882-1890) with a septuagenarian called Mr. Mathers. It is probable that this story relates to a retired coachman called Henry Mathews (pronounced 'Mathers' in the Devonian vernacular). He was the uncle of Henry Mathews Baskerville who drove BFR and ACD about Dartmoor in 1901. Indeed, English Census records reveal that Henry Baskerville and 75 year-old Henry Mathews resided together in Ipplepen during 1891.

During December 1905, *The Windsor Magazine* commenced publication of a series of 12 articles that were principally written by BFR and collectively entitled *Chronicles in Cartoon: A Record of our Own Times.* The first of these articles was numbered and entitled *I – Royalty* (Vol. 13, pp. 35-51) and it is accompanied by an editorial footnote that reads as follows:

BERTRAM FLETCHER ROBINSON

The foregoing article is the first of

AN IMPORTANT SERIES

In which, under this general title, practically

ALL THE CARTOONS OF CELEBRITIES

Which have appeared in

"VANITY FAIR"

Will be, for the first time, grouped together and republished, in the original colours. Ensuing articles will cover the realms of

THE CHURCH THE POLITICAL WORLD LITERATURE
THE ARMY THE NAVY SPORT SOCIETYART
MUSIC SCIENCE THE STAGE FINANCE

And every phase of public life invaded by the famous Cartoonists of "Vanity Fair".

The remaining 11 episodes were entitled: *II. Potentates, Princes and Presidents, III. Politics: First Series, IV. Politics: Second Series* (with Wilfrid Meynell), *V. Bench and Bar, VI. The Army* (with Evan Ashton), *VII. Music, VIII. Cricket* (with Home Gordon), *IX. Rowing, Games, and Athletics, X. Empire-Builders, XI. Science and Medicine* (with Charles R. Hewitt), *XII. Explorers and Inventors.* This serialization ran to 215 pages and features some 250 caricatures by Carlo Pellegrini and Leslie Ward. These include Guy Nickalls, William H. Grenfell, Charles Burgess Fry and Rudolph Chambers Lehmann (see Plate 73), each of whom had worked with BFR during his early writing career (see Chapters 3 & 4). BFR wrote the narrative that interconnects and often expands upon the short biographies that were originally scribed by 'Jehu Junior'.

134

Plate 73. R. C. Lehmann (1895) by Leslie Ward ('Spy').

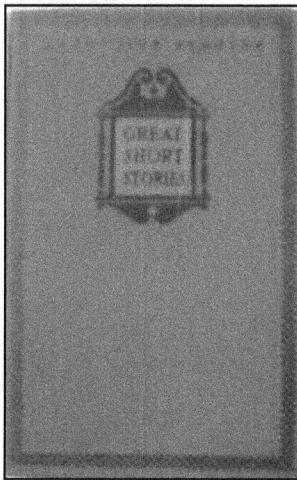

Plate 74. *Great Short Stories, Volume 1 (1):*
Detective Stories (1906).

During 1906, P. F. Collier & Sons of New York published
an anthology entitled *Great Short Stories, Volume 1 (1):*
Detective Stories (see Plate 74). It was edited by one

135

BERTRAM FLETCHER ROBINSON

William Patten and features 12 stories written by Broughton Brandenburg (1), Arthur Conan Doyle (2), Anna Katherine Green (1), Edgar Allen Poe (3) and Robert Louis Stevenson (4). The 12th and final story is *The Vanished Millionaire* by BFR and it is preceded by the following introduction:

> Fletcher Robinson is a London Journalist, the editor of "Vanity Fair," and author of a dozen detective stories in which are recorded the startling adventures of Mr. Addington Peace of Scotland Yard. He collaborated with Conan Doyle in "The Hound of the Baskervilles." When some of these stories appeared in the American magazines, for an unexplained reason (presumably editorial) the name of the hero was changed to Inspector Hartley.

It is worth noting that during 1903, an American editor called Norman Hapgood persuaded ACD to 'resurrect Holmes' for a series of 13 short stories that were each first published in *Collier's Weekly*. Like *Great Short Stories, Volume 1 (1): Detective Stories*, this periodical was produced by the Irish-born publisher, Peter Fenelon Collier. Clearly, Collier had close ties with ACD and presumably sent him an advanced copy of the book. ACD raised no objection to the comment that links BFR with *The Hound of the Baskervilles*, which implies that he remained content to endorse BFR's work.

On 7th June 1906, BFR had a story entitled *The Mystery of Mr. Nicholas Boushaw* published by *Vanity Fair*. In this 9th Addington Peace story, the detective locates the body of a missing man inside a recently dug grave. BFR recorded in a footnote to this story, that a real-life murderer had concealed the body of his victim in this way and that the body went undiscovered for 11 years. The story is set within a fictional village called 'Crone' in Dorset. The description of Crone bears a closer resemblance to Newton Abbot than to anywhere in Dorset. There is also an interesting reference to a nearby location called 'Heatree' in the story. There is no village or town called Heatree in Dorset or anywhere else in England, but there is a Heatree House on the edge of Dartmoor. Henry Baskerville later claimed that 'Haytree House' was the model for 'Baskerville Hall' in *The Hound of the Baskervilles* (see Chapter 11).

On 14th July 1906, 66 year-old Emily Robinson died at Springfield Nursing Home in Newton Abbot. BFR's mother was buried in the same plot as Joseph Fletcher Robinson at St. Andrew's Church. The burial service was conducted by The Revd R. D. Cooke. Thereafter, BFR commissioned Charles Eamer Kempe to design a commemorative stained-glass window that depicts the Good Shepherd with St. Peter and St. Paul. This window was added to the north-side of the Chancel at St Andrew's Church, opposite the memorial window dedicated to her husband. On 28th July of that same year, Emily's estate was proved at £17,679 17s 5d gross, and Sidney Hacker was awarded probate. Emily's Last Will and Testament was witnessed by both Sidney Hacker and Harold Michelmore. BFR was named as the principal beneficiary and he inherited Park Hill House Estate.

BERTRAM FLETCHER ROBINSON

On 18th October 1906, it appears that both BFR and ACD attended a meeting of 'Our Society' at the home of Max Pemberton. The host delivered a paper entitled *An Attempt to Blackmail Me*. Two days later, BFR played a round of golf with ACD and three others at Hindhead in Surrey. This meeting is recorded as an entry in the personal diary of ACD's brother, Captain John Francis Innes Hay Doyle (affectionately referred to as 'Innes').

On 24th October 1906, BFR (see Plate 75) had an article entitled *The Gathering of the Government, Or, How They Loved Each Other* published by *Vanity Fair*. This was his final contribution to that journal. Shortly thereafter, he resigned the editorship of *Vanity Fair* and this position passed to Frank Harris (1907-1911). By November of that same year, BFR was appointed 'Editor' of a weekly periodical called *The World, a Journal for Men and Women*. It was managed by Max Pemberton and owned by Lord Northcliffe (see Plate 76). '*The World*' was founded during 1874 by Edmund Hodgson Yates and Eustace Clare Grenville Murray, but the former man quickly became the sole editor and proprietor. It mainly published society news, literary comment and gossip.

Plate 75. BFR (circa 1906).
COURTESY OF THE TOPFOTO COLLECTION.

Plate 76. Alfred Harmsworth.
(1st Viscount Northcliffe).

Chapter 9

Early Death

On Tuesday 13th November 1906, BFR visited the office of a solicitor called W. E. Crimp at 17 Essex Street, Westminster, London. He made his Last Will and Testament and appointed both Gladys Robinson and Harold Gaye Michelmore, to act as joint 'Executors and Trustees'. BFR's will was witnessed by Crimp and a journalist called Charles Thomas from Kingston-upon-Thames. The document reveals that BFR had recently relocated to 44 Eaton Terrace, Belgravia, London (see Plate 77). This property was constructed around 1884 and it was run for nearly 20 years as a lodging house by one Henry Purchase. In 1903 it was sold to one Walter E. Evans-Jones, a Fellow of the Royal Geographical Society of London. It was Evans-Jones who subsequently sold 44 Eaton Terrace to BFR during 1906. It is probable that BFR's decision to write, or rewrite, his will was prompted by this move and by the changes to his financial circumstances following his recent appointment to the editorship of *The World*.

Between Saturday 8th December 1906 and Sunday 23rd December 1906, BFR visited The Paris Automobile Exhibition at the Grand Palais (see Plate 78). It was the 9th such annual event to be organised by the Automobile Association of France. It is probable that BFR met-up with a journalist called Major C. G. Matson (pseudonym 'Nostam') because the latter man had three related articles published in The World on the 11th, 18th and 25th of December 1906. During September 1936, Max Pemberton wrote that during this trip, BFR 'spent a merry evening, awoke in the middle of the night with a terrible thirst, and was so very foolish as to drink from the water-bottle in his bedroom. Of course, he got typhoid, and died in a few days' (see Chapter 10).

Plate 77. 44 Eaton Terrace.

Plate 78. The Grand Palais in Paris (circa 1900).

141

BERTRAM FLETCHER ROBINSON

On Tuesday 11th December 1906, *The World* published a literary supplement entitled *Boot and Stocking Fund Supplement*. It announced that BFR had recently completed a story entitled *An Episode of 1746: Being the Unchivalric Conduct of an Irish Gentleman*. The following month, it was published under the revised title of *How Mr Denis O'Halloran Transgressed His Code* in an American periodical called *Appleton's Magazine*. This was the final item that BFR had published during his life-time and it was his 55th short story.

On Wednesday 16th January 1907, BFR's close friend and former flatmate, Percy Holden Illingworth MP, married one Mary Mackenzie Coats at St. James's Church, Paisley, Renfrewshire, Scotland. There is no indication that BFR attended this ceremony despite the fact that Illingworth had attended BFR's marriage and acted as a 'Witness'. This apparent absence, might suggest that BFR was too ill to travel at that time. Ironically, on 3rd January 1915, 45 year-old Illingworth also died from typhoid after eating a 'bad oyster'.

During the early hours of Monday 21st January 1907, 36 year-old BFR died at 44 Eaton Terrace. The death certificate states that he died from 'Enteric Fever 21 days. Perforation of intestine. Peritonitis 24 hours.' Enteric, or typhoid, is caused by a bacterium that is frequently transmitted by the ingestion of food or water contaminated by the faeces of an infected person. These bacteria then multiply in the blood and migrate to the digestive tract. In 1907, there were no antibiotics available and the mortality rate for 'untreated cases' was between 10% and 30%. Fatal cases typically present with 3 stages of symptoms that each last approximately 1 week: slow rising temperature, high fever with delirium and intestinal perforation/hemorrhage. It is worth noting that *The Times* newspaper reported that in the 4 weeks preceding BFR's death, there were some 8,500 deaths recorded in London and these included 26 cases of enteric. Furthermore, in the week preceding BFR's death, the Metropolitan Asylum and London Fever Hospital reported 108 new cases of enteric. Hence, BFR's illness ran a classic course and would have been readily diagnosed by any London-based physician.

BFR's death was certified by Dr. Henry Menzies (1867-1936). He was educated at St. Paul's School, West Kensington, London and Jesus College, Cambridge (1886-1894). Menzies was awarded a Bachelor of Arts degree in Natural Science (1889), a Bachelor of Medicine degree (1894) and a Bachelor of Surgery degree (1894). Menzies then worked as a 'Resident House Physician', 'Assistant House Surgeon' and 'Assistant Surgical Registrar' at nearby St. George's Hospital. He also worked as a 'Clinical Assistant' at Great Ormond Street Hospital for Sick Children. Later, Menzies retained a position as 'Anaesthetist' at St. George's Hospital and was elected a member of The West London Medical and Chirurgical Society. Thus, he was a well-qualified, experienced and respectable clinician (see Chapter 11).

BERTRAM FLETCHER ROBINSON

Plate 79. 4 Ashley Gardens.

Plate 80. Jesus College 1st XI Cricket Team (circa 1890) featuring Henry Menzies (1st row & 2nd from right).
COURTESY OF THE PATRICK CASEY COLLECTION.

144

BERTRAM FLETCHER ROBINSON

At the time of BFR's death, Menzies also ran a private practice from his home at 4 Ashley Gardens (1897-1918). This property (see Plate 79) is located just 50 meters from 126 Ashley Gardens where BFR frequently stayed with Trevor Lewis and Percy Illingworth (1895-1901). It appears likely that Menzies was well acquainted with both BFR and Illingworth because all 3 men were members of the Jesus College Cambridge Society and they overlapped in their studies there. Indeed, Menzies had co-founded the JCCS and was secretary at the time of BFR's death. Furthermore, like BFR and Illingworth, Menzies was a distinguished sportsman and regularly represented Jesus 1st XI Cricket Team (see Plate 80). Between 1891 and 1893, he also played first-class cricket as a wicket-keeper/batsman for Middlesex. During one county game, played at Crystal Palace, he stumped the famous England test batsman and captain, Dr. William Gilbert Grace.

On Tuesday 22nd January 1907, John Philip Claude Morris, registered BFR's death at St. George Registry Office, Hanover Square, Belgravia, London. The death certificate correctly recorded BFR's occupation as 'Journalist and Editor' but his name was mistakenly listed as 'Bernard Fletcher Robinson'. Such clerical errors were inevitable because there were some 300 deaths per day in London at that time. Claude was BFR's brother-in-law and the death certificate reveals that he was working as an 'Assistant Clerk' for the Royal Navy at nearby 'HMS Resolution in Chatham'. It appears that he witnessed BFR's death whilst providing support to Gladys. That same day, obituaries were published in *The World*, *The Times* and *Daily Express* newspapers. The latter, included the following comments:

BERTRAM FLETCHER ROBINSON

It was his remarkable versatility that made Mr. Fletcher Robinson so conspicuous a success as a journalist. It is no disparagement of the many brilliant Contributors to the daily newspapers to call him the best descriptive writer of the day. He was interested in most subjects, from the serious problems that agitate all humanity to the topics of the passing hour, and he wrote brilliantly about all...In his spare moments Mr. Robinson collaborated with Sir A. Conan Doyle in 'The Hound of the Baskervilles,' wrote many thrilling detective stories and edited a series of volumes on sport. He was also the author of the popular political song 'John Bull's Store,' that was sung all over England a few years ago...Few men had a larger circle of friends. His was the sunniest and most delightful of natures. He was a charming companion, a witty conversationalist and a most loyal colleague...and he will be much missed in the world of politics, literature and sport.

At 9am on Thursday 24th January 1907, BFR was conveyed by GWR train from Paddington to Newton Abbot (see Plate 81). Records made by the funeral director reveal that his body was interred inside a 'lead coffin', built about a 'pine shell' and enclosed inside a 'best oak case'. At 2.40pm that same day, the coffin was transferred by 8 pallbearers to a glass-sided hearse. It then made its way to St. Andrew's Church in Ipplepen via Newton College and Park Hill House. The hearse was followed by a cortege comprising of 1 'Brougham carriage', several 'buses' and 5 'Landau carriages'. One bus contained only floral tributes and it had to make a return journey to the railway station to collect more. The funeral service began at 3.30pm and it was jointly conducted by The Revd R. D. Cooke and The Revd R. W. Manneer (headmaster at Newton College). Amongst the many mourners were Richard Robinson (see Chapter 1), Mrs. Holt (aunt), Claude Morris, Harold Michelmore and Henry Baskerville. It was reported that Gladys 'travelled as far as Newton Abbot, where she stayed the night in the company of Lady Harmsworth'. The congregation sang the hymn Fight the Good Fight and Peace, Perfect Peace. The inscription on BFR's headstone (see Plate 82) reads as follows:

**IN
LOVING MEMORY OF
BERTRAM FLETCHER
ROBINSON,
THE BELOVED HUSBAND OF
GLADYS HILL ROBINSON,
OF PARK HILL, IPPLEPEN,
WHO DIED 21ST JANUARY 1907,
AGED 36 YEARS,
"DO WELL, O LORD: UNTO THOSE THAT
ARE GOOD AND TRUE OF HEART."**

BERTRAM FLETCHER ROBINSON

At 4pm on Thursday 24th January 1907, The Revd
Septimus Pennington conducted a memorial service for
BFR at St. Clement Danes Church, The Strand, London.
The congregation included Arthur Hammond Marshall,
Owen Seaman, Max Pemberton, Cyril Arthur Pearson,
Percy Everett, Lord Northcliffe, Sir Joseph Lawrence
(former Conservative MP and a co-founder of the Tariff-
Reform League), Sir Felix Sermon (Laryngologist), Sir
William Bell (former member of the British Iron Trade
Association and tax-reform campaigner), Anthony Hope
Hawkins (novelist and playwright), Clement King Shorter
(journalist and author), Gerald Fitzgerald Campbell
(journalist and author) Leslie Ward ('Spy'), Thomas
Anstey Guthrie (journalist and author), Leonard Upcott Gill
(journalist, author and publisher), John Evelyn Leslie
Wrench (journalist and author), Henry Hamilton Fyfe
(journalist and editor), and Charles Thomas (witness to
BFR's Last Will and Testament). This assembly also sang
Peace, Perfect Peace. It should be noted that ACD was
unable to attend either the funeral service, or the memorial
service, because at that time, he was busily campaigning for
the release from prison of one George Edalji who had been
convicted of cattle maiming during 1903.

Plate 81. Newton Abbot Railway Station (circa 1906).

BERTRAM FLETCHER ROBINSON

Plate 82. BFR's headstone.

On Friday 25th January 1907, *The Western Morning News* newspaper reported that 'The news of Mr. Robinson's death caused a profound impression at Ipplepen, where his family will always be remembered with affection'. This same article reports that the following messages had accompanied floral tributes that were delivered to the funeral service at St. Andrew's Church on the previous day:

To my dear husband, in loving memory
[Gladys Robinson].

In affectionate remembrance from Mr and Mrs O. R. Robinson.

[BFR's cousin and the son of the late Sir John Robinson].

BERTRAM FLETCHER ROBINSON

In ever affectionate memory and with deepest sympathy from his cousin, Emily Robinson.

[Daughter of the late Sir John Robinson].

With love and sympathy from Dulcie and Claude.

[sister-in-law and brother-in-law].

From Mr. and Mrs. Percy Everett and his little Godchild, Winn. God bless you then until we meet again.

[The parents of BFR's goddaughter].

With deep sympathy from Lord and Lady Northcliffe.

[BFR's employer at the time of his death].

In affectionate remembrance of an old friend, from Mr. Trevor Lewis, 126 Ashley Gardens, London, SW1.

[BFR's friend and former flatmate at that same address].

In loving memory of an old and valued friend from Arthur Conan Doyle.

[BFR's friend and author of *The Hound of the Baskervilles*].

In loving memory and kind remembrance from Miss Jessie Pope, Regent's Park Road, Finchley.

[BFR's friend and a noted writer].

BERTRAM FLETCHER ROBINSON

From 'Our Society,' with deepest regrets from fellow members.

[The criminology society to which, BFR, ACD and Pemberton each belonged].

In loving remembrance of dear Fletcher Robinson, from the staff of 'The Observer' Office – revered as a colleague and loved as a friend. From the staff of The Daily Express.

With deepest sympathy and warmest regard from the staff of The World, to its late Editor.

Thereafter, BFR's name was added to the dedication on the stained-glass window that is installed in the Chancel of St. Andrew's Church. He had recently commissioned this window to commemorate his mother, Emily Robinson, who died on 14th July 1906. This full inscription reads as follows:

"To the glory of God and in ever loving
memory of Emily Robinson, who entered
into rest xivth July mcmvi aged lxvii
years; this window is the gift of her son
Bertram Fletcher Robinson who only
Survived her six months."

On Saturday 26th January 1907, obituaries appeared in *The Western Guardian*, *The Sphere*, *The Athenaeum*, *The Illustrated London News*, *The Mid-Devon and Newton Times*. On that same day, the *Daily Express* reported upon the memorial service that was held for BFR at St. Clement Danes Church. This article ends with a short eulogistic

BERTRAM FLETCHER ROBINSON

poem that was written by Jessie Pope (1868-1941). She wrote for *Punch*, the *Daily Express* and *Vanity Fair* but is perhaps best remembered for her pro-WWI poetry. It is said that Pope's war-poems provoked Wilfred Owen to write his famous poem, *Dulce et Decorum Est*. Her tribute to BFR reads as follows:

> Good Bye, kind heart; our benisons preceding,Shall shield your passing to the other side. The praise of your friends shall do your pleading In love and gratitude and tender pride.

> To you gay humorist and polished writer, We will not speak of tears or startled pain. You made our London merrier and brighter, God bless you, then, until we meet again!

On Wednesday 30th January 1907, the undertakers sent an invoice for £97 2s 9d plus £1 2s 6d to 44 Eaton Terrace (invoice number: '16089'). It was marked for the attention of BFR's solicitor and oldest friend, Harold Gaye Michelmore (see Chapter 2). On that same day, Michelmore wrote and sent the following letter to another client:

Dear Miss Taylor

Your telegram was forwarded to me at Chudleigh last night and I can not tell you how sorry I am to hear of your Aunts' death. I know that she was getting up in years but when last I saw her she looked so well and was obviously

152

devoted to Miss Trimble and yourself that I am sure the death must be a great shock to you both.

I am just starting for London in connection with the death of one of my oldest friends Mr. Fletcher Robinson the editor of the World whose death you may have noticed in the paper last week but if I can be of assistance to you in your sorrow before the funeral I will return at once. I had arranged to stay at 49 Wimpole Street W [Westminster] and a telegram there will find me at once.

I have appointments until Monday [4th February] when I intended coming back but if I can help you please send me a wire and I will cancel them until next week and come back. In any event please let me know when and where the funeral will be as I should like to attend it if I can under the circumstances.

I should cancel my visit so I can and not start were it not that Mr. Robinson's Widow who is distinctly in much sorrow is expecting me.

Yours most sincerely,

Harold G. Michelmore.

BERTRAM FLETCHER ROBINSON

On Saturday 16th February 1907, BFR's estate was proved at £35,949 3s 0d net and Michelmore was granted probate. This sum amounted to more than twice the value of the estate that BFR had inherited from his mother just 6 months earlier. Evidently, BFR was solvent and had made a comfortable living both as a writer and editor. Gladys was named as the principal beneficiary to BFR's estate. However, he also bequeathed £2,000 each to Michelmore and several cousins (the sons of Mrs. Holt née Hobson from Birkenhead). BFR also gave £1,000 in-trust to Newton Abbot Hospital for a 'Fletcher Robinson Bed' and £2,000 in-trust to Newton College Proprietary College for a 'Fletcher Robinson Modern Languages Scholarship'. The latter bequest was due to be paid upon the death of Gladys but the school shut before she died and so this wish was never executed.

On Thursday 28th February 1907, Michelmore and Claude Morris officially corrected the name recorded on BFR's death certificate from 'Bernard Fletcher Robinson' to 'Bertram Fletcher Robinson'. Shortly thereafter, further obituaries were published in *The Book of Blues* and the *1907 Annual Report* of the Jesus College Cambridge Society.

Chapter 10

Death Aftermath

During May 1907, a BFR article was published posthumously in an American periodical entitled *Munsey's Magazine*. The title of this piece is *People Much Talked About in London – The Prominent Men and Women whose Names are most frequently Heard in the World's Metropolis – an Interesting Procession of Celebrities, Political, Military, Naval, Literary, and Social – their personalities* (Vol. 37, no. 2, pp. 135-145). This article includes the following footnote:

> This is one of the last articles written by the author before his death, which occurred a few months ago. Mr. Robinson had recently been appointed editor of the London *World* [sic]. He was a rising figure in English journalism.

Hence, it appears that BFR wrote this article during the Autumn of 1906. In it, he profiles many of the most prominent British personalities during the Edwardian era. It is illustrated with 20 portrait photographs that include the politicians Arthur Balfour, Sir Henry Campbell-Bannerman, Winston Churchill and Keir Hardie. BFR also discusses the literary figures of George Bernard Shaw, H. G. Wells, Rudyard Kipling and ACD. He describes the latter man thus (pp. 142-143):

> In Pall Mall, too, it is likely that we shall meet some of the more famous of English literary

men bound for that most exclusive of clubs — the Athenaeum. Here comes that kindly giant, Sir Arthur Conan Doyle, the creator of Sherlock Holmes, prince of detectives. He is of a fine British type, a clear-headed, sport-loving, big-hearted patriot.

A mention of the Athenaeum Club reminds me of a story Sir Arthur told me of his first visit, after election, [8th March 1901], to that home of the respectabilities. He walked up to the hall-porter and, desiring to introduce himself to that important person's notice, asked if there were any letters for Conan Doyle. Now the Athenaeum is a favorite resort of the clerical dignitaries, and the hall-porter, who had small acquaintance with literature, replied 'No, canon, there are no letters for you.'

Sir Arthur did not care to explain, and for some weeks he suffered much from the disapproving eye of the hall-porter. The suit of tweeds affected by the great novelist shocked that functionary deeply, and when one day Sir Arthur appeared in a long racing-coat, the spectacle had such an effect upon him that Doyle had to rush to the desk and explain that he was not a dignitary of the church, but a writer of tales to whom some latitude in dress might be allowed.

Sir Arthur is an earnest supporter of the rifle-club movement. He has erected targets for a

miniature rifle-range at his house on the moors
at Hindhead. There you may observe groom and
carpenter, mason and village blacksmith
competing against one another on a Saturday
afternoon in the same fashion as their forebears
did with 'The Long' bow, winning Creçy and
Agincourt thereby. Among them the novelist
may be seen at his best, shooting with them,
cheering them on with kindly words or
awarding prizes, chiefly out of his own pocket.

BFR's description of the 'Saturday afternoon' rifle meets at
ACD's home is detailed and it might imply that he had
witnessed such an event. Between 1897 and 1907, ACD
lived in a house called 'Undershaw' at Hindhead in Surrey.
During late-1900, he set aside an area of his grounds as a
firing-range and founded the Undershaw Rifle Club. It is
feasible that BFR and ACD attended a rifle meet there after
their trip to Hindhead Golf Course on Saturday 20th October
1906 (see Chapter 8). In any event, it is clear that BFR was
well disposed towards ACD prior to his death.

On 31st July 1907, Max Pemberton sent an advanced copy
of his new novel entitled *Wheels of Anarchy* to an unknown
recipient (see Plate 83). It contains a handwritten
inscription that is both signed and dated by the author (see
Plate 84). The story is an adventure tale about anarchists
and assassins that is set throughout Europe. The novel's
hero, Mr. Bruce Driscoll, a recent Cambridge graduate,
appears to be partly modelled upon BFR. Driscoll is the
personal secretary to a rich and mysterious philanthropist,
Jehan Cavanagh, who actively opposes political radicalism.
The first book edition was published by Cassell &

BERTRAM FLETCHER ROBINSON

Company Limited of London during 1908. In 1909, that same company republished it as a 'Sixpenny Novel'. In both cases, the story is preceded by the following 'Author's note':

> This story was suggested to me by the late B. Fletcher Robinson, a dear friend, deeply mourned. The subject was one in which he had interested himself for some years; and almost the last message I had from him expressed the desire that I would keep my promise and treat of the idea in a book. This I have now done, adding something of my own to the brief notes he left me, but chiefly bringing to the task an enduring gratitude for a friendship which nothing can replace.

This statement is important for several reasons. Firstly, it shows that BFR made contributions to the plot of another story that was written by a popular author of the day. Secondly, it reveals that BFR was lucid during the early phase of his illness and that he had anticipated the possibility of death. Evidently, this period was short because the notes that he wrote for Pemberton were 'brief'. This in turn suggests that BFR experienced a period of delirium before he died and was unable to work. Such observations are consistent with the course of typhoid.

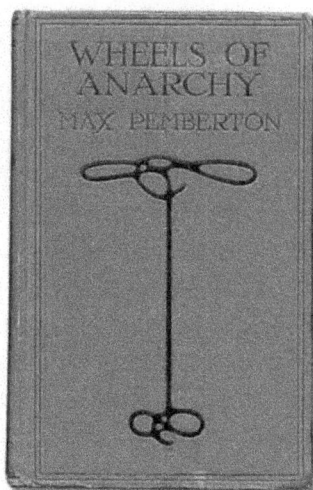

Plate 83. *Wheels of Anarchy* (1907).

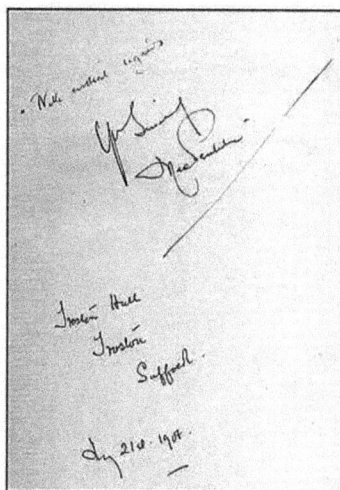

Plate 84. Pemberton's inscription.

BERTRAM FLETCHER ROBINSON

On 18th September 1907, ACD married Jean Leckie at St. Margaret's Church, Westminster, London. The couple then held a wedding reception at the nearby Hôtel Métropole. The guest-list included Max Pemberton and the recently pardoned ex-prisoner, George Edalji. The former man was evidently well acquainted with both ACD and BFR. This adds weight to the claims that he later made in relation to the events that surrounded the inception of *The Hound of the Baskervilles* (see Chapter 6). The latter man's freedom was partly due to the tireless campaigning that ACD had commenced just prior to BFR's death. This likely explains why ACD was unable to attend either BFR's funeral service or memorial service.

Plate 85. Front-cover of *Pearson's Magazine* (August 1909).

BERTRAM FLETCHER ROBINSON

Plate 86. The 'Unlucky Mummy'
(serial no. EA 22,542).

During August 1909, a writer called G. St. Russell had an article entitled *The Mysterious Mummy* published in *Pearson's Magazine* (see Plate 85). In his article, Russell chronicles the events that surrounded the acquisition of a mummy-board by the British Museum during 1889 (see Plate 86). This coffin-lid was found at Thebes in Egypt and it is believed to have been made for a woman of high rank around 950BC. Her identity is unknown but the artefact is frequently referred to as either 'The Lady of the College of Aman-Ra' or 'Priestess of Amen-Ra' (see Plate 86). It has also been called the 'Unlucky Mummy' because of superstitions that link it to various misfortunes that include BFR's death. Russell explains the connection between this coffin-lid and BFR's death as follows (pp. 163-165):

161

BERTRAM FLETCHER ROBINSON

About the middle of the 'sixties [1860's] a party of five friends went in a dahabia for a trip up the Nile. They went to Luxor, on their way to the Second Cataract, and there explored Thebes, with its temple to Amen-Ra, unequalled on earth in its ruined magnificence.

A well-known English lady of title entertained the party, and the Consul, Musaph Aga, gave a fête in their honour. One night the consul sent to his friends an Arab, who reported he had just found a mummy case of unusual worth. Next morning he brought the case for inspection. It was seen to picture a woman's face, of strange beauty, but of a cold malignity of expression. The case was bought by one of the party, Mr. D., who, however, agreed to draw lots with the others for possession of the treasure; and the case passed to a friend, whom we may call Mr. W.

From that time its history has been clearly traced - a history marked by an uncanny series of fatalities, which appear not to have ceased, even after the case found its abode among a thousand similar relics.

On the return journey of the party, one of the members was shot accidentally in the arm by his servant, through a gun exploding without visible cause. The arm had to be amputated. Another died in poverty within a year. A third was shot. The owner of the mummy case found, on reaching Cairo, that he had lost a large part of his fortune, and died soon afterwards.

The priestess of Amen-Ra was showing her displeasure in a convincing manner. When the case arrived in England, it was given by its owner, Mr. W., to a married sister living near London. At once misfortune fell upon her household; large financial losses were suffered, bringing other troubles with them.

But before this, one day the Theosophist, Mme. Blavatsky, entered the room in which the case had been placed. She soon declared there was a most malignant influence in the room. On finding the cover, she begged her hostess to send it away, declaring it to be a thing of utmost danger. The lady, however, laughed at this idea as a foolish superstition.

Presently she sent the case to a well-known photographer in Baker Street. Within a week he called upon her in great excitement, to say that while he photographed the face with the greatest care, and could guarantee that no one had touched either his negative or the photograph, the photograph showed the face of a living Egyptian woman staring straight before her with an expression of singular malevolence. Shortly afterwards the photographer died suddenly and mysteriously.

BERTRAM FLETCHER ROBINSON

About this time Mr. D. happened to meet the owner of the coffin lid, and, hearing her story, begged her to part with it; and she sent it to the British Museum. The carrier who took it died within a week, and the man who assisted him met with a serious accident.

This is the history as it was verified - with the exception of the last statement - by one who for three months was at pains to gather the tangled threads of the evidence, and gained proofs of the identity of all those who suffered from the anger of the priestess - the late Mr. B. Fletcher Robinson. We have told the story very much as he told it; and he declared that every one of the facts was absolutely authentic. He himself seems to have thought that when the mummy case arrived at the Museum, and was installed in a place of honour [First Egyptian Room], the series of fatalities had ended, for he wrote:

"Perhaps it is that the priestess only used her powers against those who brought her into the light of day, and who kept her as an ornament in a private room, but that now, standing amongst queens and princesses of equal rank, she no longer makes use of the malign powers which she possesses."

But a lady, Mrs. St. Hill, who recently delivered a lecture in London, in which she told the story, remarked that not long after Mr. Fletcher

164

Robinson had recorded the facts, he himself
died at an early age, after a brief illness.

BFR researched the 'Unlucky Mummy' over a 12 week
period that spanned his move between the *Daily
Express* and *Vanity Fair* (1904). Later, Arthur Hammond
Marshall wrote that after BFR joined *Vanity Fair* 'he told
me a wonderful tale about a mummy, which had caused the
death of everybody who had had to do with it...I don't
know whether he ever wrote the story.' It therefore appears
that BFR's comments in relation to the 'Unlucky Mummy'
were merely ideas for the plot of some unpublished tale.
Nevertheless, around 1909, interest in both Spiritualism and
Occultism was growing in London and Mrs. St. Hill's
lecture evidently struck a chord with the chattering classes.
This might explain why during that same year, Gladys
elected to sell both 44 Eaton Terrace and Park Hill House to
William Maxwell and Sidney King Eldridge respectively.
She then appears to have emulated both her late father and
husband by paying an extended visit to continental Europe.

On 13th February 1911, it appears likely that ACD visited
The Royal Geographical Society in London and attended an
illustrated lecture entitled *Further Exploration in Bolivia.*
This lecture was delivered by the South American explorer
and Old Newtonian, Major Percy Harrison Fawcett.
Thereafter, Fawcett provided some assistance to ACD with
his adventure story entitled *The Lost World* that was first
serialized in *The Strand Magazine* during 1912 (see
Chapter 2). Perhaps Fawcett's connection with Newton
College and the recent gossip about the 'Unlucky Mummy',
reminded ACD about BFR? In any event, the tale's
narrator, Edward E. Malone, has much in common with

BERTRAM FLETCHER ROBINSON

BFR. For example, both BFR and Malone spent part of their 'boyhood' in the West Country, shot, fished and exceeded 6 feet in height. Furthermore they each became accomplished rugby players, London-based journalists and loved a woman called Gladys.

On 15th April 1912, *RMS Titanic* sank with the loss of 1,517 lives after striking an ice-berg off the coast of Newfoundland. This news was received with incredulity throughout both Britain and America. Over the ensuing weeks, there was a proliferation of theories and tales that sought to explain the loss of this 'unsinkable' ship. It was even suggested that the accident was caused by the transit of the coffin-lid belonging to the 'Priestess of Aman-Ra'. However, records reveal that it was on display at the British Museum at the time of the sinking. Nevertheless, such tales may have minded a British journalist and writer, Douglas Brooke Wheelton Sladen (1856-1947), to write the following comments about BFR in his 1913 autobiography entitled *Twenty Years of My Life* (New York: E.P. Dutton & Company Publishers):

> The popular account of his death is that, not believing in the malignant powers of the celebrated mummy case in the British Museum, he determined to make a slashing attack on the belief in the columns of The Daily Express [sic], and went to the museum, and sent his photographer there, to collect materials for that purpose: that he was then, although in the most perfect health, struck down mysteriously by some malady of which he died.

Evidently, BFR was still a topic of conversation some 6 years after he died. It also appears that Sladen (see Plate 87) did not himself subscribe to the 'popular account' about the circumstances surrounding his death. This is significant because Sladen was acquainted with BFR and his friends, ACD (see Plate 88), Rudolph Chambers Lehmann, Barry Pain and Max Pemberton. Indeed, Sladen writes in his autobiography that 'I well remember the first time I went to the Pemberton's, before he had moved to Fitzjohn's Avenue [circa 1900]. It was a Sunday evening, and he had asked us to meet poor Fletcher Robinson, who would have been one of the greatest journalists of the day had he survived'. Clearly, London-based writers moved in small social circles and it is telling that not one of them ever reported a conflict between BFR and ACD (see Chapter 11).

THE AUTHOR
Drawn by Yoshio Markino

Plate 87. Douglas Sladen by Yoshio Markino.

BERTRAM FLETCHER ROBINSON

SIR A. CONAN DOYLE
Drawn by Yoshio Markino

Plate 88. ACD by Yoshio Markino.

During the 1st World War (1914-1918), Gladys met a Royal Artillery officer called Major William John Frederick Halliday (affectionately referred to as 'Fred'). He was born in London during 1882 and was educated at Orley Farm School near Harrow-on-the-Hill in Middlesex. Interestingly, the main school building was originally called 'Julians' but it was renamed after it was discovered that Anthony Trollope had lived there and referred to it in his novel, *Orley Farm* (1862). On 7th January 1918, William and Gladys were married in France (see Plate 89):

HALLIDAY : ROBINSON.—On the 7th Jan., 1918, at the British Embassy. Paris, Major William John Frederick Halliday, D.S.O.. R.F.A., to Mrs. Gladys Fletcher Robinson, daughter of the late Mr. Philip Morris. R.A.

Plate 89. A marriage announcement from *The Times* newspaper (15th January 1918).

It is perhaps a measure of the grief that Gladys evidently felt about BFR's death that she should have elected to wait for almost 11 years before remarrying. Ironically, this second marriage took place in the very same city where BFR had contracted the disease that led to his death. Thereafter, the newly-weds relocated to 'Northend', 82, St. Mark's Road, Henley-on Thames, Oxfordshire.

On 28th March 1921, the 'Unlucky Mummy' again made the news following a recent reorganisation at the British Museum (see Plate 90). The reference to 'Mr. Stead' is particularly interesting because one William Thomas Stead had died aboard the *RMS Titanic*. He was a British journalist, spiritualist and founder of the *Review of Reviews* (1890). He was also well acquainted with ACD and had acted as both his 'collaborator and combatant'. Allegedly, shortly before the ship sank, Stead and 7 other passengers assembled in the first-class smoking-room. The only survivor from that group, Fred Seward, reported that Stead had related a story about an Egyptian coffin-lid that bore an inscription that when read aloud, led to death. This tale has clear parallels with the story that BFR had conceived in relation to the 'Unlucky Mummy'. Indeed, it may have been the same story because BFR also appears to have known Stead. During 1904, BFR and PG Wodehouse co-wrote a satirical playlet for *Vanity Fair* that is entitled *Our*

BERTRAM FLETCHER ROBINSON

Christmas Pantomime – Little Red Riding Hood; or, The Virtuous British public and the Smart Set Wolf (8th December 1904, pp. 731-734). In this item, the character of the 'Good Fairy' is played by 'W. T. Stead'.

> **" UNLUCKY MUMMY."**
>
> The galleries contain, of course, many things familiar to those who have studied the collection in the past, but the number of objects now to be seen for the first time is very large. Thus in the First room there is an interesting collection of anthropoid coffins which are anterior to the 17th dynasty and carry the series some 300 or 400 years farther back historically: Close at hand is a not less interesting basket burial, with the bones of the buried person visible. It may be noted in passing that a change has been made in the place assigned to the Lady of the College of Amen-Râ (No. 22,542). This is the so-called " unlucky mummy," about whom many stories have been circulated without any foundation. It was said by all sorts of people that anyone who interfered with her would meet with calamity, and the late Mr. Stead predicted that if any further attempt was made to move the lady it would probably result in the utter destruction of the whole room, such was the virulent nature of the priestess as revealed to him by her astral body. Although she has been moved to another place in the Wall-case none of the dire results so confidently foretold are yet known to have occurred. Specialists will note some extremely interesting additions to the series of coffins from Barsha, in Upper Egypt.

Plate 90. A report from *The Times* newspaper (28th March 1921).

BERTRAM FLETCHER ROBINSON

On 3rd April 1923, ACD arrived in New York to commence a 4-month lecture tour of North America on the topic of Spiritualism. He had declared his conversion to that religion during November 1916, in an article entitled *A New Revelation. Spiritualism and Religion* that was published by the psychic magazine, *Light.* It is possible that ACD was minded of BFR by his recent voyage and the relatively recent article about the 'Unlucky Mummy' in *The Times* newspaper. In any event, on 7th April 1923, he was attributed with the following claims in relation to BFR's death by an anonymous correspondent from the *Daily Express* newspaper:

> ...it was caused by Egyptian "elementals" guarding a female mummy, because Mr Robinson had begun an investigation of the stories of the mummy's malevolence. "It is impossible to say with absolute certainty if this is true," said Sir Arthur to me today. "If we had proper occult powers we could determine it, but I warned Mr Robinson against concerning himself with the mummy at the British Museum. He persisted, and his death occurred....I told him he was tempting fate by pursuing his enquiries...The immediate cause of death was typhoid fever, but that is the way in which the elementals guarding the mummy might act. They could have guided Mr Robinson into a series of such circumstances as would lead him to contract the disease, and thus cause his death - just as in Lord Carnarvon's case, human illness was the primary cause of death...

Evidently, ACD also linked BFR's death to the research that he had undertaken at the British Museum in relation to the 'Unlucky Mummy'. It is interesting to note that ACD tried to discourage BFR from pursuing that research. This might suggest that ACD had prior knowledge about the subject of BFR's investigation. Interestingly, during 1891, ACD visited the British Museum to conduct some research and thereafter wrote a short story entitled *Lot No. 249*. This story is about a student who acquires a mummy at auction and then uses it to murder his enemies. It was published in *Harpers Magazine* during January 1892. Leaving aside ACD's views about the supernatural, it is worth noting that he too asserted that BFR was killed by typhoid. He was an expert on this condition, having previously witnessed an epidemic at first-hand whilst serving as a volunteer physician during the 2nd Boer War (see Chapter 5).

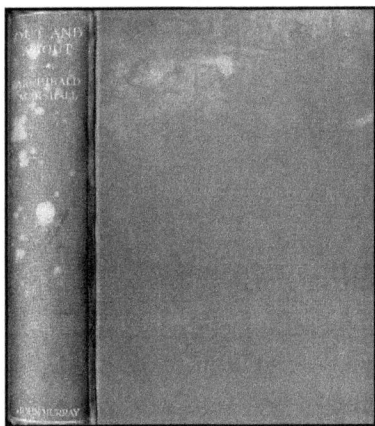

Plate 91. *Out and About: Random Reminiscences* (1933).

BERTRAM FLETCHER ROBINSON

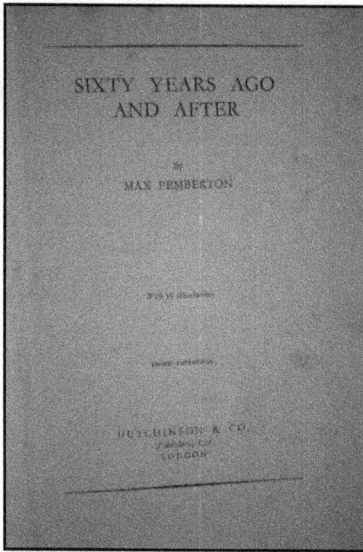

Plate 92. Title page of *Sixty Years Ago and After* (1936).

On 14th June 1933, BFR's friend, Arthur Hammond Marshall had an anecdotal autobiography entitled *Out and About: Random Reminiscences*, published under his pen name of 'Archibald Marshall' (London: John Murray). In Chapter 1 of his book (see Plate 91), Marshall describes his time as an undergraduate at Trinity College, Cambridge. Thereafter, he also makes the following comments in relation to BFR's death (pp. 4-5):

> I didn't see so much of Bobbles after we had both married and I was living in the country, but wrote occasionally for Vanity Fair, which was his last editorship [sic]. The very last time I saw him he told me a wonderful tale about a mummy, which had caused the death of everybody who had had to do with it. He was

BERTRAM FLETCHER ROBINSON

collecting his material, already had enough for a sensational story, and was on the track of more. This story is now well known, and I have seen frequent references to it, but this was the first I had heard of it. I don't know whether he ever wrote the story, but it cannot have been long after that he was dead himself. He had gone over to Paris, caught pneumonia, and died in a few days at the age of thirty-six or seven. Not for a long time afterwards did I connect his death in my mind with that story about the mummy, and I have never heard of anyone else who did so.

Both BFR and Marshall were married within a few months of one another during the summer of 1902. They then settled with their wives in London and Beaulieu in Hampshire respectively. It is interesting to note that Marshall was unaware of the earlier speculation that linked BFR's death to a 'mummy', or that he was editor of *The World* when he died. For these reasons, his suggestion that BFR died from 'pneumonia' should be regarded as either a mistake or oversight. On 29th September 1934, 68 year-old Arthur Hammond Marshall died suddenly in Cambridge.

During September 1936, BFR's friend, now Sir Max Pemberton, had an anecdotal autobiography published by Hutchinson & Company Limited of London (see Plate 92). Its full title is *Sixty Years Ago and After, Sporting Reminiscences, Memoirs of days at Cambridge and as a journalist. London in the eighties and famous personalities of those days.* Pemberton makes references to BFR's work at *Cassell's Magazine* during his editorship. He also makes the following comments in relation to BFR's death (p. 125):

> Alas, poor Fletcher Robinson, he went to the Paris Exhibition, spent a merry evening, awoke in the middle of the night with a terrible thirst, and was so very foolish as to drink from the water-bottle in his bedroom. Of course, he got typhoid, and died in a few days.

It might be recalled that Pemberton was the manager of *The World* at the time that BFR was appointed as its editor. He was also a keen motorist and presumably sanctioned BFR's fateful trip to the Paris Automobile Exhibition. In any event, Pemberton reflected that his death was 'greatly lamented' and that it resulted from typhoid. It is interesting to note that he makes no reference to BFR's links with either *The Hound of the Baskervilles* or the 'Unlucky Mummy'. This suggests that he felt that neither matter warranted any further comment. However, it will be recalled that his recollections about the former matter were subsequently published in an article by the London *Evening News* newspaper on 25th May 1939 (see Chapter 6). On 22nd February 1950, 86 year-old Sir Max Pemberton died at his home in London.

On 8th January 1946, 66 year-old Gladys Hill Halliday died from 'pulmonary failure' at her home in Henley-on Thames. Two days later, her death was announced in *The Times* newspaper (see Plate 93). On 14th June 1946, the estate of Gladys Hill Halliday was proved at £23,779 8s 3d net and probate was awarded to BFR's friend, Harold Gaye Michelmore. Her husband, Major William John Frederick

Halliday, was the sole beneficiary. Gladys also stipulated that, upon his death, any residue should pass to a nephew called Lieutenant-Commander Peter Withers. Gladys never bore any children of her own.

> HALLIDAY.—On Jan. 8, 1946, suddenly, at Northend, St. Mark's Road, Henley. GLADYS, dearly loved wife of MAJOR F. HALLIDAY, D.S.O.

Plate 93. A death announcement from
The Times newspaper (10th January 1946).

> MAJOR W. J. F. HALLIDAY AND MISS H. MACNAMARA
> The engagement is announced between Major William John Frederick (Fred) Halliday, D.S.O., late Royal Artillery, of 82, St. Mark's Road, Henley-on-Thames, and Honor Macnamara, of 15, Gordon Place, London, W.8, youngest daughter of the late Mr. and Mrs. H. V. Macnamara, formerly of Ennistymon House, County Clare, Ireland.

Plate 94. A forthcoming marriage announcement from
The Times newspaper (12th September 1946).

> HALLIDAY : MACNAMARA.—On Nov. 5, 1946, quietly, in London, MAJOR W. J. F. HALLIDAY, of 82, St. Marks Road, Henley-on-Thames, to HONOR MACNAMARA, of 15, Gordon Place, London, W.8.

Plate 95. A marriage announcement from
The Times newspaper (15th November 1946).

During September 1946, just 9 months after Gladys had died, 63 year-old Major Halliday became engaged to 47 year-old Honor Nesta Macnamara (see Plate 94). On 5th

November of that same year, the couple were married in London (see Plate 95). Thereafter, it is not known what became of Major Halliday. However, it is known that on 21st July 1986, Honor Nesta Halliday died aged 87 years in Berkshire.

During March 1957, Harold Gaye Michelmore died aged 86 years at Newton Abbot in Devon. He was a highly respected local solicitor and had acted as a legal representative to BFR's family for nearly 50 years. Hence, there is no reason to doubt Michelmore's assertion that BFR had contributed to the plots of 2 Sherlock Holmes stories that were written by ACD (see Chapter 6). Moreover, he never queried the official cause of BFR's death (see Chapter 11). The following item is Michelmore's listing in the 1934 edition of *Who's Who in Devonshire* (Hereford: Wilson & Phillips):

MICHELMORE, Harold Gaye. Solicitor. Saffron Close, Chudleigh. Born 1870, Newton Abbot. Son of late Henry Michelmore. Educated at Newton College. Married 1905, Margaret Mignon, daughter of late Dr. Alfred Lewis Galabin. Officer of St. John of Jerusalem; President of Newton Abbot, and Vice-President Chudleigh St. John Ambulance Brigades; Chairman, Newton Abbot Society for Prevention of Cruelty to Animals; Member Of Council of All England Lawn Tennis Association; Chairman, Devon County Lawn Tennis Association; President Torquay, President Newton Abbot, and Vice-President

BERTRAM FLETCHER ROBINSON

Teignmouth Lawn Tennis Clubs; Vice-President, Devon Squash Rackets Association; President, Newton Corinthian Football Club; President, Newton Abbot and District Canine Society; President, Newton Abbot and District Fanciers' Society; formerly President, now Vice-President, Newton Abbot Fat Stock Society; President, Newton Abbot (Stover) Golf Club; President of Bovey Tracey and District Agricultural Association; Honorary Director, Newton Abbot Races; Local Director, Commercial Union Assurance Company; Member Dart Board of Conservators; Hon. Secretary, Lower Teign Fishing Association; President, Newton Abbot Chamber of Commerce. Devon County Lawn Tennis Champion, 1894-1914. Recreations-Fishing, Shooting, Tennis, and Squash Rackets. Heir-Alfred Philip Galabin Michelmore (1906).

Chapter 11

Authorship Controversy

The 1st of 9 monthly episodes of *The Hound of the Baskervilles* was published by the British edition of *The Strand Magazine* during August 1901. The following month the same serialization was commenced in the American edition of that same periodical. The 1st episode in each edition was accompanied by a footnote that attributed the credit for the 'inception' of the story to BFR. Even before each serialization was concluded it was speculated that he had written much of the published narrative. Perhaps this explains why subsequent acknowledgements in both the 1st British and American book editions sought to dilute BFR's involvement? In any event, it is important to emphasise that BFR himself, never claimed to be anything more than the 'assistant plot producer' (see Chapter 6). Nevertheless, the extent of his involvement with the narrative is still contested. This chapter aims to trace the origins of this authorship controversy.

During October 1901, the 2nd instalment of *The Hound of the Baskervilles* was published in the American version of *The Strand Magazine*. Shortly thereafter, the following remarks appeared in a monthly American literary magazine entitled *The Bookman*:

> Every one who read the opening chapters of the resuscitation of Sherlock Holmes in the September number of the Strand Magazine

must have come to the conclusion that Dr. Doyle's share in the collaboration was a very small one. The Hound of the Baskervilles opens very dramatically, and promised to be a good tale. But the Sherlock Holmes to whom we are introduced is a totally different personage from the Sherlock Holmes of The Study in Scarlet [sic], The Sign of Four, The Adventures and The Memoirs. Of course all the little superficial tricks and mannerisms have been worked in, but there it ends. In a brief note Dr. Doyle, whose name alone is at the head of the story, acknowledges the collaboration of Mr. Fletcher Robinson. Of course the matter is one which concerns primarily only the two authors and their publishers: but we have very little hesitation in expressing our conviction that the story is almost entirely Mr. Robinson's and that Dr. Doyle's only important contribution to the partnership is the permission to use the character of Sherlock Holmes.

This article was probably written by one of the two joint-editors, Arthur Bartlett Maurice (1873-1946), because he later by-lined an article that returned to the topic of authorship. This further item was published shortly after the release of the 1st American book edition of *The Hound of the Baskervilles* (15th April 1902). In that later article, Maurice echoed the earlier comments, albeit in a slightly more circumspect manner:

BERTRAM FLETCHER ROBINSON

When the subject of this story was first discussed in literary and publishing circles in London there prevailed the idea that Mr. Fletcher Robinson had in hand a story to which Dr. Doyle was lending some assistance, his name, and the character Sherlock Holmes. A little later it was being said that Dr. Doyle and Mr. Robinson were in collaboration on this new Sherlock Holmes story. Finally, the first instalment of the tale itself appeared as being the work of Dr. Doyle alone. Allusion to Mr. Fletcher Robinson was made only in a foot-note, in which the reputed writer courteously, but rather vaguely, thanked Mr. Robinson for one or two hints and suggestions that had been of some value to him in the writing the story. Just what the meaning of all this was, just how much Mr. Robinson did contribute to the inception and the working out of *The Hound of the Baskervilles*, the reviewer is neither inclined nor prepared to say.

During June 1902, *The Bookman* published a story entitled *The Bound of the Astorbilts*. It is an early parody of *The Hound of the Baskervilles* and it was written by an American called Charlton Andrews (1878-1939). Andrews' concluded this work with the following comments:

As I gazed, from far out upon the moor there came the deep, unearthly baying of a gigantic hound. Weirdly it rose and fell in blood-curdling intensity until the inarticulate sound gradually shaped itself into this perfectly distinguishable wail: "I wonder how much of it Robinson wrote?"

It should be stressed that *The Bookman* had acquired a reputation for publishing literary gossip under Maurice's joint editorship (1899-1909). Furthermore, it was frequently flippant in respect to the work of British authors. For example, during December 1903, it published a satirical pastiche by Charlton Andrews that is collectively entitled *The Resources of Mycroft Holmes: Solver of Historical Mysteries* (Vol. 18, no. 4, pp. 365-372). This work comprises of 3 separate items entitled: *I. He Repudiates Sherlock, II. He Solves the Mystery of the Shakespearian Authorship, III. He Solves the Mystery of the Man in the Iron Mask.* Hence, the foregoing serious of remarks and allegations might be dismissed as self-serving rumour mongering. It is perhaps telling, that neither Maurice nor Andrews queried ACD's authorship of *The Hound of the Baskervilles* beyond June 1902, despite the fact that their respective careers continued for several decades thereafter.

On 2nd February 1949, *The Western Morning News* newspaper published a review of John Dickson Carr's biography entitled *The Life of Sir Arthur Conan Doyle* (London: John Murray). This article refers to ACD's connections with Devon and it contains a number of factual errors and omissions. These in turn, prompted Harold Michelmore, The Revd Henry Robert Cooke and Henry Baskerville (see Plate 96) to write '*Letters to the Editor*' (Noel Vinson). On 16th February 1949, 78 year-old Baskerville had the following letter published in *The Western Morning News*:

Sir – I feel sure that Mr. H. G. Mitchelmore [sic] has given the most accurate account of the whole subject of "The Hound of the Baskervilles." [see Chapter 6]. I was coachman for the Robinson family for 20 years. I also have in my possession the first book that was published, autographed by Bertram Fletcher Robinson and with apologies for using my name. In that edition is Conan Doyle's thanks to Robinson for his help in getting all the detail.

I fetched Conan Doyle from Newton Abbot Station and brought him to Parkhill, Ipplepen, when he came to join his friend Robinson with a view to visiting parts of Dartmoor to get the threads of the story. I also drove them to Bovey Tracey (which is mentioned in the book as Coombe Tracey), Hound Tor, Haytree (which is Baskerville Hall), and Grimspound.

The following is a copy of Conan Doyle's thanks to Robinson: "My dear Robinson,—It was to your account of a Westcountry legend that this tale owes its inception. For this and for all your help in all the details all thanks.—Yours most truly, A. Conan Doyle."

H. M. (HARRY) BASKERVILLE.

Ashburton, Feb. 9.

This is Baskerville's first published comment in relation to *The Hound of the Baskervilles*. It should be noted that at this time, he did not claim that BFR contributed directly to the narrative of the story. However, following the death of his wife, Alice (27th May 1951), Baskerville's story began to evolve. On 17th October 1951, a newspaper entitled *The South Devon Journal* published an article entitled *His Name Has Gone Down In Mystery – Harry Baskerville*. In this article, Baskerville claimed that ACD had asked him for permission to use his name in the story. On 1st November 1957, (just 8 months after Michelmore's death), a newspaper entitled *The Western Times and Gazette* published an article entitled *A Devon Coachman Whose Name Has Become Immortal*. In this article, Baskerville claimed that BFR and ACD had directly sought his assistance with the plot for *The Hound of the Baskervilles*. Finally, on 16th March 1959 (just 3½ months before Hammer Films released the first colour version of *The Hound of the Baskervilles*), Baskerville was attributed with the following comments in an article that was written by Peter Evans for the *Daily Express*:

> Doyle didn't write the story himself. A lot of the story was written by Fletcher Robinson. But he never got the credit he deserved. They wrote it together at Park Hill, over at Ipplepen. I know because I was there...Mr. Doyle stayed for eight days and nights. I had to drive him and Bertie [BFR] about the moors. And I used to watch them in the billiards room in the old house, sometimes they stayed long into the night, writing and talking together...Then Mr. Doyle left and Bertie said to me: "Well, 'Harry', we've finished that book I was telling you about. The one we're going to name after you."

BERTRAM FLETCHER ROBINSON

The letter written by ACD to his mother from the Duchy Hotel in Princetown (see Chapter 6) suggests that he intended to spend no more than a single night at Ipplepen (Sunday 2nd June 1901). Moreover, given that ACD played cricket at 11.30am in Sherborne in Dorset on Monday 3rd June (72 miles from Ipplepen), it is unlikely that he would have felt inclined to work into the small hours of that morning. Hence, Baskerville's claims in relation to BFR's involvement with *The Hound of the Baskervilles* are at best unreliable. It has been suggested that Baskerville deliberately overstated both his own involvement and that of BFR in order to gain publicity for himself. On 28th March 1962, Baskerville died aged 91 years, at his home in Ashburton. Shortly thereafter, obituaries were published in various newspapers including *The Western Morning News* (30th March), the *New York Herald Tribune* (2nd April) and *The New York Times* (2nd April). Hence, it appears that Baskerville did indeed secure a degree of notoriety for himself as he had evidently intended.

Plate 96. Henry Baskerville (1955).

BERTRAM FLETCHER ROBINSON

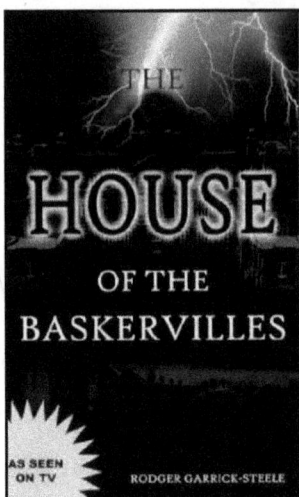

Plate 97. *The House of the Baskervilles* (2003).

On 2nd September 2000, *The Western Morning News* published an article in which, it is asserted that BFR wrote the entire narrative for *The Hound of the Baskervilles*. This claim is attributed to a 'former psychologist' called Rodger Garrick-Steele and it led to worldwide media interest. On 20th October 2003, Garrick-Steele elaborated upon his theory within a print-on-demand book entitled *The House of the Baskervilles* (see Plate 97). In this 624 page book, Garrick-Steele claimed that ACD and Gladys committed adultery and then conspired to poison BFR in order to conceal the former man's plagiarism! However, it should be noted that ACD's sole authorship of the story was announced in *Tit Bits* prior to his research trip to Dartmoor with BFR in May/June 1901. Furthermore, following the publication of the story, BFR and ACD regularly socialised and the former man wrote in high praise of the latter man on at least 3 separate occasions (see Chapter 8). Finally, none of BFR's numerous friends ever referred to any friction between him and ACD. Hence, ACD had no motive to kill BFR and there is no reason to doubt that the latter man's death was due to anything other than complications stemming from typhoid. Indeed, it is probable that BFR's physician and fellow Jesuan, Dr. Henry Menzies, was particularly attentive to his patient's condition (see Plate 98).

The remarks made by Maurice, Andrews, Baskerville and Garrick-Steele are wholly unwarranted. All the evidence suggests that ACD and BFR had fully intended to write a Dartmoor-based story together whilst aboard the *S.S. Briton* in July 1900. The theme for this story was settled upon during a subsequent visit to Cromer in late April 1901. Shortly thereafter, ACD introduced the character of Sherlock Holmes and also wrote the 1st instalment for *The Hound of the Baskervilles*. During late May and early June 1901, BFR and ACD conducted research for the story together in Devon. Clearly, by this stage, the two men had agreed that ACD alone should write the narrative. However, why was BFR seemingly content to withdraw from a full collaboration and instead act as a mere 'assistant plot producer'?

The answer to this question may never be unequivocally resolved. However, it is conceivable that BFR felt that Sherlock Holmes was the intellectual property of ACD and therefore decided to limit his involvement upon the introduction of this character to the story. Alternatively, there are indications that BFR was unable to co-author the narrative for a number of professional reasons. For example, he had some 14 items published in the *Daily Express* and *Pearson's Magazine* during the 16-week period when ACD was writing the narrative for *The Hound of the Baskervilles* (May 1901–September 1901). Furthermore, he had already been commissioned to edit a book entitled *Ice Sports* for *The Isthmian Library* and also to write 25,000 words of 'descriptive letterpress' for a book entitled *Sporting Pictures* (see Chapter 12). Finally, during 1901, BFR was living with his aged uncle Sir John Robinson and it appears that he was assisting him with his autobiography (see Chapter 8).

Additionally, BFR commenced a courtship with Gladys Morris during 1901 that ultimately led to their marriage on 3rd June 1902. Throughout this period BFR's prospective father-in-law, Philip Morris was struggling to keep his young family whilst battling a chronic illness that ultimately contributed to his death (22nd April 1902). It seems highly probable that BFR would have paid regular visits to their nearby home at 92 Clifton Hill, St Marylebone, London, in order to assist Philip, Gladys and her two younger siblings in whatever way he could. Similarly, BFR must have been mindful of his own father's growing infirmity and it appears that he made frequent trips to Ipplepen prior to Joseph's death on 11th August 1903.

So it appears that for the aforementioned professional and personal reasons, BFR was content to assist ACD with the plot of *The Hound of the Baskervilles* but not its narrative. Indeed, ACD confirmed as much during June 1929 when he wrote the following statement in a preface to a collection of four Sherlock Holmes novellas entitled *The Complete Sherlock Holmes Long Stories* (London: John Murray):

BERTRAM FLETCHER ROBINSON

Then came The Hound of the Baskervilles. It arose from a remark by that fine fellow, whose premature death was a loss to the world, Fletcher Robinson, that there was a spectral dog near his home on Dartmoor. That remark was the inception of the book, but I should add that the plot and every word of the actual narrative are my own.

Nevertheless, BFR is deserving of some gratitude for the role he played in inspiring ACD to resurrect Sherlock Holmes who had been 'killed-off' during 1893. ACD subsequently wrote 32 short stories and 1 novella featuring Sherlock Holmes, but none ever surpassed the popular success of *The Hound of the Baskervilles.*

Plate 98. Overleaf (pp. 190-192). Obituary for Henry Menzies from *The JCCS Annual Report* (1936).

BERTRAM FLETCHER ROBINSON

Among the many famous members of the College who have passed on, none will be more missed than Dr. Henry Menzies, who died at the age of 68 on March 7th, 1936, after a life devoted to a noble but exacting profession. His illness, which he so courageously bore, was primarily due to that devotion.

Dr. Menzies came up in 1886, after winning a Natural Science Scholarship. He subsequently took the degrees of B.A., M.B. and B.Ch. He was a member of the *Natives* and *Rhadegunds*, and for four years he was a distinguished member of the College XI, at a time when Jesus cricket was at its zenith, the team including, amongst other Blues, such famous men as Sam Woods, Gregor McGregor and A. J. L. Hill. Later he played for Middlesex, often deputising as wicket-keeper for McGregor himself. On one such occasion he achieved the rare distinction of stumping W. G. Grace (on the Crystal Palace ground). An eye witness thus described the incident :—

" W.G. stepped right out of his ground and missed a short-pitched 'un, but God was with Henry and it was all beard and bails, and W.G. was out ! " It has been said that Menzies' appeal could have been heard at Westminster.

But Dr. Menzies' chief claim to honour amongst Jesus men, is that he was the founder of the Jesus College Society. Its inception dates back to the first night of the Varsity cricket match in 1896, when fourteen old Jesus men dined together at the Junior Athenæum Club. As the direct

BERTRAM FLETCHER ROBINSON

result of this dinner, the Society was successfully launched in 1903, Dr. Menzies being elected Honorary Secretary, an office which he held until his death. Under his indefatigable Secretaryship, the Society has gradually increased in numbers, until now over 1,400 invitations to the annual dinner are despatched. Many generations of Jesus men owe a deep debt of gratitude to Dr. Menzies for the opportunities which these dinners afford of meeting their contemporaries, especially those who may be home from abroad on leave, or on holiday, as well as those who have been helped by the Society.

Only those who have been in close touch with the Jesus College Society continuously for a long period, can begin to estimate what he did for it and how much it meant to him. It is hardly an exaggeration to say that Dr. Menzies *was* the Society. Always at the dinner, until exiled from it last year by illness, always unsparing in his own efforts for its success, always too generously grateful for any small help that he had from anyone else, always too modest even to make the speech that we all used to call for, he had (we may hope) an annual reward in those unique gatherings at the Trocadero or the Café Royal whither the very spirit of the College was for the time being transported.

Menzies was a man of few words, but he compressed in them a wealth of good sense and playful irony. He shunned the limelight, but could not escape popularity. He did not conceal his aversion from shams and bores, for he was himself the soul of sincerity and unselfishness.

BERTRAM FLETCHER ROBINSON

29

His manner sometimes appeared to be gruff (perhaps that was the origin of his nickname Blucher) but this endeared him to us, for it hid a heart of gold.

Jesus men of all ages who knew Dr. Menzies well enough to secure his friendship valued it more than they could show. It was, perhaps, not too easy to win, but it was well worth winning. Dr. Menzies was not a man to bandy meaningless compliments. There was a fine edge to his irony and, when he wished, he could be devastating. But no kinder or more loyal man ever lived ; and for Jesus men he had but one standard : devotion to the College. It was, of course, devotion to the College itself which inspired his service to the Society. He loved to come up and walk round the College on a Sunday morning in the May Term, to dwell on the unique beauty of its setting, on its distinguished past, on his care for its present reputation, on his passionate ambition for its future. His was an outstanding example of the affection which, more than most in Oxford and Cambridge, our College knows how to arouse and to retain.

Some of us will miss bitterly his frequent, brisk little notes of congratulation and rebuke and suggestion. We remember that it was in great part his vigour and his generosity, which, a few years ago, put the Jesus College Society in its present enviable financial position. The Society is itself his best memorial, the memorial that he would value most.

Chapter 12

BFR BIBLIOGRAPHY

During April 1961, a magistrate from Toronto called S. Tupper Bigelow had a 1,100-word article entitled *The Singular Case of Fletcher Robinson* published in *The Baker Street Gasogene* (Vol. 1, No. 2, pp. 19-22). During 1993, it was republished in *The Baker Street Briefs* (pp. 70-72) by the Metropolitan Reference Library in Toronto. In his article, Bigelow makes the following comments in relation to BFR:

> Except for the various dedications of *The Hound of the Baskervilles*, Fletcher Robinson appears to be virtually unknown. One hunts in vain for any mention of him in *The Oxford Companion to English Literature*, *The Reader's Encyclopedia*, *The Encyclopedia Britannica* and *The Columbia Encyclopedia*, and he apparently said nothing worthy of note on record, as he is not mentioned in either Bartlett's *Familiar Quotations* or *The Oxford Dictionary of Quotations*. So he was a literary non-entity, except for the single fact that he was the inspiration for the best Sherlock Holmes story ever written, which entitles him, it seems to me to be posthumously knighted (if, indeed, he is dead) beatified, and later on, if things go well, canonized.

Bigelow wrote these comments in the wake of the claims that were made by Henry Baskerville either side of the release of the 1959 Hammer Films version of *The Hound of the Baskervilles* (see Chapter 11). The absence of any entries in relation to BFR within the reference volumes is indeed correct. However, the assertion that he was 'a literary non-entity' is patently incorrect. In fact, between 1892 and 1907, he wrote 265 items (750,000 words) that featured in 15 periodicals and 8 books. Furthermore, he held 6 editorial positions with *The Newtonian* (1887-1889), *The Granta* (1893-1895), *The Isthmian Library* (1897-1901) [8 books], *Daily Express* (1900-1904), *Vanity Fair* (1904-1906) and *'The World'* (1906/1907). BFR's work has also been republished 27 times.

The remaining pages of this chapter list all the items that BFR is **known** to have written or edited. It does not include any leaders or items that he may have written under other pseudonyms. Also excluded is a playlet entitled *The Progressive's Progress* that BFR reportedly co-authored with PG Wodehouse shortly before his death. Where the date of publication cannot be ascribed to either a given day or month, it has been listed at the beginning of the relevant year. It should also be noted that each title is written as it appears in the original publication.

The following abbreviations in square brackets denote:

[ar] = article;
[ss] = short story;
[pm] = poem;
[pl] = playlet;
[ly] = lyric.

BERTRAM FLETCHER ROBINSON

1887-1889

BFR edited issues 98 - 115 of Volumes 13 and 14 of his school magazine entitled *The Newtonian*. This periodical was produced by a local printer and stationer called G.H. Hearder of Wolborough Street in Newton Abbot and was periodically collated and leather-bound.

1893:

18th February.	*The Granta*: A Compromise [pm] (p. 210).
22nd April.	*The Granta*: A Chess Player's Chortle [pm] (p. 265).
6th May.	*The Granta*: A Craven Attack [pm] (p. 302).
15th June.	*The Granta*: Chuck Her Up! [pm] (p. 395).
14th October.	*The Granta*: The Female Extensionist [pm] (pp. 10-11).
14th October.	*The Granta*: Spectator Inops [pm] (p. 15).
21st October.	*The Granta*: A Quid Pro Quo [pm] (p. 29).

1894:

20th January	*The Granta*: "How To Be Happy Though Married" [pm] (p. 133).
20th January.	*The Granta*: A Memory [pm] (p. 143).
27th January.	*The Granta*: To The Muse Of Poetry [pm] (p. 149).

BERTRAM FLETCHER ROBINSON

10th February	*The Granta*: An Appeal [pm] (p. 187).

10th February   *The Granta*: An Appeal [pm] (p. 187).

3rd March.   *The Granta*: Solvitur Ambulando [pm] (pp. 236-237).

28th April.   *The Granta*: Scene Elysium [pl] (pp. 278-279).

28th April.   *The Granta*: A Woman's Revenge [pm] (pp. 283-284).

26th May.   *The Granta*: A Protest [pm] (p. 348).

3rd November.   *The Granta*: To An Old Friend [pm] (pp. 36-37).

1895:

16th November   *The Granta*: Irish Beauties Of The Last Century [pm] (p. 76).

1896:

October.   Robinson, B.F., (ed. Pemberton, M.), *Rugby Football*, (London: A.D. Innes & Co.).

1897:

23rd January.   *The Granta*: Ye Ancient Ballade [ly] (p. 144).

March.   *Cassell's Family Magazine*: A Day With The Hounds [ar] (pp. 355-364).

April.   *Cassell's Family Magazine*: The New Railway To London [ar] (pp. 492-500).

April.	Pemberton, A.C. & others, (ed. Robinson, B.F.), *The Complete Cyclist*, (London: A.D. Innes & Co.).
June.	*Cassell's Family Magazine*: Through The Flames [ar] (pp. 42-50).
July/August.	*The Railway Magazine*: The Great Railway Extension [ar] (Vol. 1).
November.	Winn, R.A., (ed. Robinson, B.F.), *Boxing*, (London: A.D. Innes & Co.).
24th November.	Lehmann, R.C., (ed. Robinson, B. F.), *Rowing*, (London: A.D. Innes & Co.).
27th November.	Budd, A.J. & Fry, C.B., *Football*, (London: Lawrence & Bullen) [with contributions by Bertram Fletcher Robinson].
December.	*Cassell's Magazine*: Capitals At Play - St. Petersburg [ar] (pp. 18-29).

1898:

January.	*Cassell's Magazine*: Capitals At Play - Copenhagen [ar] (pp. 178-187).
February.	*Cassell's Magazine*: Capitals At Play - Berlin [ar] (pp. 227-236).
March.	*Cassell's Magazine*: Capitals At Play - The Hague [ar] (pp. 398-407).
April.	*Cassell's Magazine*: Capitals At Play - Vienna [ar] (pp. 496-505).
May.	*Cassell's Magazine*: Capitals At Play - London [ar] (pp. 627-637).
28th July.	McLean, D.H. & Grenfell, W.H., *Rowing & Punting*, (London:

BERTRAM FLETCHER ROBINSON

	Lawrence & Bullen) [with contributions by Bertram Fletcher Robinson].
30th September.	Smith, G.G., (ed. Robinson, B.F.), *The World of Golf*, (London: A. D. Innes & Co.).
22nd November.	Monier-Williams, M.S., (ed. Robinson, B.F.), *Figure-Skating*, (London: A.D. Innes & Co.).
December.	*Cassell's Magazine*: The Guards Of Europe [ar] (pp. 53-61).

1899:

January.	*Cassell's Magazine*: The Duke's Hounds A Chat About The Badminton [ar] (pp. 206-210).
May.	*Cassell's Magazine*: Emperors' Gardens [ar] (pp. 665-672).
June.	*Cassell's Magazine*: London Night By Night – I. The Next Day's Dinner [ar] (pp. 48-56).
July.	*Cassell's Magazine*: Black Magic – The Story Of The Spanish Don [ss] (pp. 178-189).
July.	*Cassell's Magazine*: London Night By Night – II. The Next Day's Paper [ar] (pp. 142-149).
27th July.	Williams, L.B., (ed. Robinson, B.F.), *Croquet*, (London: A.D. Innes & Co.).

August.   *Cassell's Magazine*: London Night By Night – III. On The River [ar] (pp. 313-320).

September.   *Cassell's Magazine*: London Night By Night – IV. The Next Day's Letters [ar] (pp. 404-411).

October.   *Cassell's Magazine*: London Night By Night – V. Late Suppers And Early Breakfasts [ar] (pp. 529-537).

November.   *Cassell's Magazine*: London Night By Night – VI. The Streets [ar] (pp. 632-639).

15th November.   Smith, J.N. & Robson, P.A., (ed. Robinson, B.F.), *Hockey: Historical and Practical*, (London: A.D. Innes & Co.).

December.   *Cassell's Magazine*: The Better Part Of Valour – Dedicated To All Sportsmen in Love [pm] (pp. 24-27).

December.   *Cassell's Magazine*: Famous Regiments – I. The Royal Horse Artillery [ar] (pp. 121-129).

1900:

January.   *Cassell's Magazine* – New Year's Day [pm] (p. 245).

January.   *Cassell's Magazine*: Famous Regiments – II. The Royal Dragoons [ar] (pp. 182-188).

25th January.   Robinson, B.F, & others, *Britain's Sea-Kings and Sea-Fights*, (London: Cassell & Company Limited)

	[Bertram Fletcher Robinson contributed 4/35 chapters and 139/756 pages].
February.	*Cassell's Magazine*: Famous Regiments – III. The Black Watch [ar] (pp. 310-318).
March.	*Cassell's Magazine*: Famous Regiments – IV. The Connaught Rangers [ar] (pp. 386-393).
March.	*Pearson's Magazine*: A True Story (Wherein all golfers may learn something to their advantage) [pm] (pp. 118-120).
March.	*Pearson's Magazine* (US): A True Story (Wherein all golfers may learn something to their advantage) [pm] (pp. 235-237).
April.	*Cassell's Magazine*: Famous Regiments – V. The Tenth (Prince Of Wales' Own Royal) Hussars [ar] (pp. 529-535).
May.	*Cassell's Magazine*: Famous Regiments – VI. The Corps Of Royal Engineers [ar] (pp. 610-619).
4th May.	*Daily Express*: Capetown For Empire [ar].
8th May.	*Daily Express*: In A Cape Hotel [ar].
14th May.	*Daily Express*: High Treason [ar].
16th May.	*Daily Express*: Boer Newspapers [ar].
21st May.	*Daily Express*: Puffing Billy At The War [ar].
22nd May.	*Daily Express*: Gate Of The War [ar].

26th May.	*Daily Express*: Behind The Veil [ar].
29th May.	*Daily Express*: Nursing An Army [ar].
5th June.	*Daily Express*: A Question Of Language [ar].
7th June.	*Daily Express*: Real Nurses Or Mere Trippers? [ar].
22nd June.	*Daily Express*: The Parcels Of Mr. H. Gatliff [ar].
25th June.	*Daily Express*: How I Nearly Became A Rebel [ar].
30th June.	*Daily Express*: How The Bond Promotes Peace [ar].
28th September.	*Daily Express*: The Danger In South Africa [ar].
8th October.	*Daily Express*: In Kruger's Pavilion [ar].
11th October.	*Daily Express*: That Censor Again [ar].
19th November.	*Daily Express*: Riding To Hounds [ar].
December.	*Pearson's Magazine*: The Sarcastic Caddie [pm] (pp. 614-616).
December.	*Pearson's Magazine* (US): The Sarcastic Caddie [pm] (pp. 646-650).
5th December.	*Daily Express*: American Slang [ar].
26th December.	*Daily Express*: About Bullies [ar].

1901:

4th January.	*Daily Express*: Is Cape Colony In Danger? [ar]

6th February.	*Daily Express*: The Queen And Her Poets [ar].
18th March.	*Daily Express*: How The Yankees Advertise [ar].
22nd March.	*Daily Express*: The Fate Of The Wild Things [ar].
1st April.	*Daily Express*: A Race Worth Watching [ar].
6th April.	*Daily Express*: A Dream Of A Boat-Race [ar].
23rd April.	*Daily Express*: What Is Doing At Glasgow [ar].
24th April.	*Daily Express*: An Exhibition In The Making [ar].
May.	*Pearson's Magazine*: Big Ben And Little Ben [pm] (pp. 567-568).
1st May.	*Daily Express*: War's Brighter Side [ar].
18th May.	*Daily Express*: From The Jaws Of Death [ar].
21st May.	*Daily Express*: "Truthful Jean" On The War [ar].
29th May.	*Daily Express*: The Grim Tragedy In China [ar].
10th June.	*Daily Express*: Memories Of The May Week [ar].
19th June.	*Daily Express*: Pro-Boers, Please Note! [ar].
July.	*Pearson's Magazine*: Up the River – The Humours and Terrors of It [ar] (pp. 117 – 120).
2nd July.	*Daily Express*: The Battle On The Thames [ar].

27th July.	*Daily Express*: A Talk With Max Adeler [ar].
August.	*Pearson's Magazine*: Concerning Cricket – The Humour of the Game [ar] (pp. 228-232).
13th August.	*Daily Express*: Last Scene At Potsdam [ar].
27th August.	*Daily Express*: The Confessions Of A Pro-Boer [ar].
September.	*Pearson's Magazine*: On Card Games And Others [ar] (pp. 340-344).
October.	*Pearson's Magazine*: On Shooting [ar] (pp. 451-456).
November.	*Pearson's Magazine*: Article: The Humour of Football [ar] (pp. 564-568).
November.	*Pearson's Magazine*: Article: Deceitful Appearances - A true story of Golfers and other Virtuous Folk [ar] (pp. 591-593).
19th November.	Cook, T.A. & others, (ed. Robinson, B.F.), *Ice Sports*, (London: Ward, Lock & Co., Ltd).
30th November.	*Daily Express*: A Book Of The Moment – War as it was Under the Iron Duke [ar].
December.	*Pearson's Magazine*: Christmas Games old and new [ar] (pp. 740-744).
21st December.	*Daily Express*: A Book Of The Moment – A Peep Into the Future According to Mr. H.G. Wells [ar].

BERTRAM FLETCHER ROBINSON

1902:

January.	*Pearson's Magazine*: The Hunting of the Fox [ar] (pp. 115-120).
8th January.	*Daily Express*: According To The Prophets [ar].
February.	*Pearson's Magazine*: Concerning Golf [ar] (pp. 228-232).
28th February.	*Daily Express*: At The Saturday Supper Club [ar].
March.	*Pearson's Magazine*: Motor-Cars and Bicycles [ar] (pp. 340-344).
15th March.	*Daily Express*: A Book Of The Hour [ar].
20th March.	*Daily Express*: A Battle At The N.S.C. [ar].
24th March.	*Daily Express*: The Coronation Boat Race [ar].
April.	*Pearson's Magazine*: Sporting and Athletic Girls [ar] (pp. 452-456).
23rd April.	Robinson, B.F., (ed. Savory, E.W.) *Sporting Pictures*, (London: Cassell & Co. Ltd.).
May.	*Cassell's Magazine*: The Laughter of Dr. Marais – A Story of the Breton Coast [ss] (pp. 653-661).
May.	*Pearson's Magazine*: Concerning Yachts – A Nautical Story or Two [ar] (pp. 564-568).
June.	*Pearson's Magazine*: Croquet and Tennis [ar] (pp. 674-678).
1st July.	*Daily Express*: A Ride With Fifty Horses [ar].

BERTRAM FLETCHER ROBINSON

17th July.	*Daily Express*: The Riflemen Of An Empire [ar].
29th July.	*Daily Express*: The Man That Was [ar].
31st July.	*Daily Express*: From Friday To Monday [ar].
7th August.	*Daily Express*: The Boers At The Seaside [ar].
September.	*Pearson's Magazine* (US): Concerning Yachts – A Nautical Story or Two [ar] (pp. 950-954).
1st September.	*Daily Express*: Two Shooting Memories - A Day with a Pointer in Devonshire and a Great Partridge Drive [ar].
25th September	*The Treasury*: "A Day of My Life." No.1. – The Journalists (pp. 30-33) [ar].
30th September.	*Daily Express*: Tales For The Children [ar].
October.	*Pearson's Magazine* (US): Up the River – The Humours and Terrors of it [ar] (pp. 1067-1070).
1st October.	*Daily Express*: The Bird Of The Autumn [ar].
8th October.	*Daily Express*: A Pair Of Humorists [ar].
18th October.	*Daily Express*: The Sagacious Lieutenant [ar].
29th November.	*Daily Express*: A Play People Love [ar].
1st December.	*Daily Express*: De Wet On The War [ar].

205

December.	*Cassell's Magazine*: Ghosts and Their Funny Ways [ss] (pp. 107-110).
December.	*The Windsor Magazine*: The Trail Of The Dead: The Strange Experience Of Dr. Robert Harland (with J. Malcolm Fraser) [ss] I. The Hairy Caterpillar (pp.121-129).
13th December.	*Daily Express*: The Story Of M. Beacaire [ar].
20th December.	*Daily Express*: Where We Hold Our Own [ar].

1903:

Bertram Fletcher Robinson wrote the lyrics to a song entitled *The John Bull Store*. The music was composed by Robert Eden. The score was arranged by George W. Byng and the sheet music was published by Elkin and Co. Ltd. of London.

January.	*The Windsor Magazine*: The Trail Of The Dead – II. The Mystery Of The Lemsdorf Ham (with J. Malcolm Fraser) [ss] (pp. 264-274).
1st January.	*Daily Express*: Story Of The Brave [ar].
3rd January.	*Daily Express*: Highway To Success [ar].
8th January.	*Daily Express*: Master And The Man [ar].
17th January.	*Daily Express*: For Collectors Only [ar].

BERTRAM FLETCHER ROBINSON

23rd January.	*Daily Express*: The Acres Of Alien Shame [ar].
28th January.	*Daily Express*: A Fight At The N.S.C [ar].
February.	*The Windsor Magazine*: The Trail Of The Dead – III. The Chase In The Snow, (with J. Malcolm Fraser) [ss] (pp. 370-379).
4th February.	*Daily Express*: Pity The Pro-Boer! [pm].
4th February.	*Daily Express*: Circulation By The Million [ar].
7th February.	*Daily Express*: In The Eye Of The Public [ar].
16th February.	*Daily Express*: Alien Thief To Britisher [ar].
March.	*The Windsor Magazine*: The Trail Of The Dead – IV. The Anonymous Article, (with J. Malcolm Fraser) [ss] (pp. 477- 486).
21st March.	*Daily Express*: Where To Dine In Paris [ar].
26th March.	*Daily Express*: Talk About The Boat Race [ar].
April.	*The Windsor Magazine*: The Trail Of The Dead – V. The Ammonia Cylinder, (with J. Malcolm Fraser) [ss] (pp. 627-638).
9th April.	*Daily Express*: A Question Of Good Taste [ar].
15th April.	*Daily Express*: A Country's Resurrection [ar].

BERTRAM FLETCHER ROBINSON

28th April.	*Daily Express*: The Return Of A Hero [ar].
May.	*The Windsor Magazine*: The Trail Of The Dead – VI. The End Of The Trail, (with J. Malcolm Fraser) [ss] (pp. 734-743).
May	*Pearson's Magazine*: The Battle of Fingle's Bridge [ss] (pp. 530-536).
23rd May.	*Daily Express*: The Man In The Cage [ar].
June.	*Pearson's Magazine*: The Romance of Motor Racing [ar] (pp. 604-610).
4th June.	*Daily Express*: The China Collector [ar].
August.	*The London Magazine*: Fog Bound [ss] (pp. 47-56).
8th August.	*Daily Express*: The Great French Trial [ar].
25th September.	*Daily Express*: A Peaceful Revolution [ar].
October.	*Pearson's Magazine*: The Debt Of Heinrich Hermann [ss] (pp. 432-440).
20th October.	*Daily Express*: A Leader Of Men [ar].
29th October.	*Daily Express*: Helping A Good Cause [ar].
14th November.	*Daily Express*: The People Of The Abyss [ar].
18th November.	*Daily Express*: On The Roof Of The World [ar].
27th November.	*Daily Express*: The Food Of The Gods [ar].

December.	*Pearson's Magazine*: Cupid = Billiard Marker [pm] (pp. 585-588).
December.	*Cassell's Magazine*: Clowns [ss] (pp. 88-90).
5ᵗʰ December.	*Daily Express*: A Quarter-Mile Of Death [ar].
24ᵗʰ December.	*Daily Express*: A Champion Of British Art [ar].
28ᵗʰ December.	*Daily Express*: A Fiscal Pantomime. The Sleeping Beauty (with P.G. Wodehouse [pl].

1904:

Bertram Fletcher Robinson wrote the lyrics to a song entitled *The Little Loafer*. The music was composed by Robert Eden and the sheet music was published by Elkin and Co. Ltd. of London.

14ᵗʰ January.	*Daily Express*: The Future Of The Very Rich [ar].
22ⁿᵈ January.	*Daily Express*: Not Playing The Game [ar].
February.	Robinson, B.F. & Fraser, J.M., *The Trail of the Dead*, (London: Ward, Lock & Co., Ltd.) [also published by Langton Hall of Toronto].
9ᵗʰ February.	*Daily Express*: The Czar's Responsibility [ar].
23ʳᵈ February.	*Daily Express*: Common-Sense v. Propriety [ar].
3ʳᵈ March.	*Daily Express*: Mischief For Idle Hands [ar].

BERTRAM FLETCHER ROBINSON

10th March.   *Daily Express*: A War That Will Decide [ar].

18th April.   *Daily Express*: A True Ghost Story [ar].

21st April.   *Daily Express*: Old West Surrey [ar].

5th May.   *Daily Express*: A Question For The Nation [ar].

10th May.   *Daily Express*: The Continent And The War [ar].

13th May.   *Daily Express*: The Black Coat Fetish [ar].

19th May.   *Daily Express*: The Future Of The Nations [ar].

26th May.   *Vanity Fair*: Women of Civilisation [ar] (pp. 664-665).

31st May.   *Daily Express*: The Home Of Islam [ar].

9th June.   *Vanity Fair*: Spain and Her King – The Royal Guest of 1905 [ar] (p. 730).

14th June.   *Daily Express*: A Pagan Metropolis [ar].

15th June.   *Daily Express*: Mr. Beckles' Invention [ar].

28th June.   *Daily Express*: "Unreliability Tests" [ar].

30th June.   *Vanity Fair*: Pagan London - Miss Corelli's Libel On The Clergy [ar] (pp. 831-832).

7th July.   *Vanity Fair*: On Political Lies – A Growing Danger In British Politics [ar] (pp. 15-16).

BERTRAM FLETCHER ROBINSON

14th July.	*Vanity Fair*: For Ladies Only [pl] (p. 41).
14th July.	*Vanity Fair*: The Policy of Honesty – An Old Proverb With New Applications [ar] (p. 48).
21st July.	*Vanity Fair*: A Sensation per Diem [ar] (pp. 79-80).
28th July.	*Vanity Fair*: The Quick and the Dead – Being a Ghost Story, With Comments Thereon [ar] (p. 105).
August.	*The Lady's Home Magazine*: The Chronicles Of Addington Peace – I. The Terror In The Snow [ss] (pp. 114-127).
11th August.	*Vanity Fair*: Pity Poor Agriculture! [ar] (pp. 175-176).
18th August.	*Vanity Fair*: Out of the Depth [ar] (pp. 207-208).
25th August.	*Vanity Fair*: The Country – Second Hand [ar] (p. 240).
September.	*The Lady's Home Magazine*: The Chronicles of Addington Peace – II. Mr. Taubery's Diamond [ss] (pp. 220-230).
September.	*Pearson's Magazine*: Historic Monuments of Britain. III. The Fortress Of The First Britons. A Description of the Fortress of Grimspound, on Dartmoor [ar] (pp. 273-280).
1st September.	*Vanity Fair*: Upon Popular Agitations [ar] (pp. 271-272).

BERTRAM FLETCHER ROBINSON

8th September.	*Vanity Fair*: The God of Irony [ar] (pp. 304-305).
29th September.	*Vanity Fair:* As We Fight Elections [ar] (pp. 400-401).
October.	*The Lady's Home Magazine*: The Chronicles of Addington Peace – III. Mr. Coran's Election [ss] (pp. 326-336).
27th October.	*Vanity Fair*: The Good Old Times [ar] (pp. 527-528).
November.	*Home Magazine of Fiction*: The Chronicles of Addington Peace – IV. The Mystery Of The Causeway [ss] (pp. 431-440).
10th November.	*Vanity Fair*: "The Standard" and the New Journalism [ar] (pp. 591-592).
17th November.	*Vanity Fair*: Satire — Not Undeserved [ar] (pp. 625-626).
December.	*Home Magazine of Fiction*: The Chronicles of Addington Peace – V. The Vanished Millionaire [ss] (pp. 577-587).
December.	*Pearson's Magazine*: Legend Of Bess The Mare [pm] (pp. 719-722).
8th December.	*Vanity Fair*: Our Christmas Pantomime – Little Red Riding Hood; or, The Virtuous British Public And The Smart Set Wolf (with P.G. Wodehouse) [pl] (pp. 731-734).

BERTRAM FLETCHER ROBINSON

1905:

January.	*Home Magazine of Fiction*: The Chronicles of Addington Peace – VI. The Mystery Of The Jade Spear [ss] (pp. 79-88).
12th January.	*Vanity Fair*: The German War Scare and 'Vanity Fair' [ar] (p. 48).
19th January.	*Vanity Fair*: 'Vanity Fair' and its Critics [ar] (pp. 83-84).
26th January.	*Vanity Fair*: Russia and France – An Historic Parallel In Revolutions [ar] (p. 120).
February.	*Pearson's Magazine* (US): The Vanished Billionaire One of Inspector Hartley's Famous Cases [ss] (pp. 140-147).
2nd February.	*Vanity Fair*: False Economy [ar] (pp. 155-156).
9th February.	*Vanity Fair*: The Franco=Russian Alliance [ar] (pp. 191-192).
May.	*Pearson's Magazine*: The Mystery Of Thomas Hearne [ss] (pp. 497-507).
18th May.	*Vanity Fair*: The Pick of the Bookstall – "Rose of the World" [ar] (p. 708).
June.	Robinson, B.F., *The Chronicles of Addington Peace*, (London: Harper & Brother) [with 2 additional Addington Peace stories entitled *The Story of Amaroff the Pole* and *The Mystery of Thomas Hearne*].

BERTRAM FLETCHER ROBINSON

29th June.	*Vanity Fair*: The Discomforts of English Racing [ar] (pp. 897-898).
6th July.	*Vanity Fair*: The Problem of National Degeneracy [ar] (pp. 15-16).
27th July.	*Vanity Fair*: "The Valley of Peace" [ar] (p. 114).
17th August.	*Vanity Fair*: The Messenger Bhoys – A Political Extravaganza [pl] (p. 209).
17th August.	*Vanity Fair*: The Chronicles of Pen – I. The Tact Of Anne [ss] (p. 210).
31st August.	*Vanity Fair*: The Chronicles of Pen – II. The Unchivalric Conduct of M. Paul [ss] (pp. 275-276).
7th September.	*Vanity Fair*: The Chronicles of Pen – III. The Return Of Gilbert Hare [ss] (pp. 306-307).
21st September.	*Vanity Fair*: The Chronicles of Pen – IV. The Curious Coincidence Of The Three Sermons [ss] (pp. 373-374).
5th October.	*Vanity Fair*: Vain Tales – No. DCLXL. The Woman's Point Of View [ss] (pp. 434-435).
12th October.	*Vanity Fair*: The Chronicles of Pen – V. Mr. Mathers, Sportsman [ss] (p. 469).
November.	*Pearson's Magazine* (US): The Return of Oliver Manton [ss] (pp. 500-505).
December.	*The Windsor Magazine*: Chronicles In Cartoon – I. Royalty [ar] (pp.35-51).

7th December.	*Vanity Fair*: II. A Tale of Mystery – The Return Of Oliver Manton [ss] (pp. 733-735).
14th December.	*Vanity Fair*: A Winters Tale – King Arthur And His Court (with P. G. Wodehouse) [pl] (pp. 778-781).
28th December.	*Vanity Fair*: Vain Tales - No. DCCI – The Sentiment Of Self-Sacrifice [ss] (pp. 846-847).

1906:

Great Short Stories, Volume 1 (1): Detective Stories edited by William Patten, published by P. F. Collier & Sons of New York. This anthology (the 1st of 3 volumes) includes 12 short stories by Broughton Brandenburg (1), Arthur Conan Doyle (2), Anna Katherine Green (1), Edgar Allan Poe (3), Robert Louis Stevenson (4). The twelfth and final item is *The Vanished Millionaire* by Bertram Fletcher Robinson (pp. 411-430).

January.	*The Windsor Magazine*: Chronicles In Cartoon – II. Potentates, Princes and Presidents [ar] (pp. 261-276).
11th January.	*Vanity Fair*: Vain Tales – No. DCCIII – Love And An Election [ss] (pp. 50-51).
25th January.	*Vanity Fair*: When Labour Rules (c.1920) The Amazing Adventure Of Mr. Hiram K. Paddle [ss] (pp. 114-115).

BERTRAM FLETCHER ROBINSON

February.	*The Windsor Magazine*: Chronicles In Cartoon – III. Politics: First Series [ar] (pp. 383-398).
1st February.	*Vanity Fair*: When Labour Rules (c.1920) In the House Of Commons [ss] (pp. 145-146).
8th February.	*Vanity Fair*: Vain Tales – No. DCCVII - A Sentimental Episode [ss] (pp. 178-179).
March.	*The Windsor Magazine*: Chronicles In Cartoon – IV. Politics: Second Series (with Wilfrid Meynell) [ar] (pp. 489-506).
1st March.	*Vanity Fair*: Vain Tales – A Jest Of Fate (with Dion Clayton Calthrop) [ss] (pp. 275-276).
15th March.	*Vanity Fair*: Vain Tales – No. DCCXII - The Last Of The Mad Lindores [ss] (pp. 339-340).
29th March.	*Vanity Fair*: Vain Tales – No. DCCXIV - The Return Of "Piccadilly" [ss] (pp. 403-404).
April.	*The Windsor Magazine*: Chronicles In Cartoon – V. Bench And Bar [ar] (pp. 611-630).
5th April.	*Vanity Fair*: The New Privileged Class [ar] (pp. 431-432).
12th April.	*Vanity Fair*: Vain Tales – No. DCCXVI - Mr. Andrew Perkins– Knight Errant [ss] (pp. 466-467).
19th April.	*Vanity Fair*: Vain Tales – No. DCCXVII - The End Of The Chapter [ss] (pp. 498-499).

BERTRAM FLETCHER ROBINSON

May.	*The Windsor Magazine*: Chronicles In Cartoon – VI. The Army (with Evan Ashton) [ar] (pp. 733-752).
3ʳᵈ May.	*Vanity Fair*: Vain Tales – No. DCCXIX - Miss Bulpit's Wooing [ss] (pp. 562-563).
10ᵗʰ May.	*Vanity Fair*: Vain Tales – No. DCCXX - West Africa Comes To Town [ss] (pp. 594-595).
24ᵗʰ May.	*Vanity Fair*: Contentment [pm] (p. 656).
31ˢᵗ May.	*Vanity Fair*: Vain Tales – No. DCCXXIII - Romance And A Racing Fraud [ss] (pp. 691-692).
June.	*The Windsor Magazine*: Chronicles In Cartoon – VII. Music [ar] (pp. 35-52).
7ᵗʰ June.	*Vanity Fair*: Wastminster Vair [ly] (p. 721).
7ᵗʰ June.	*Vanity Fair*: Vain Tales – No. DCCXXIV - The Mystery Of Mr. Nicholas Boushaw [ss] (pp. 725-726).
14ᵗʰ June.	*Vanity Fair*: How We Entertain [pl] (pp. 756-757).
21ˢᵗ June.	*Vanity Fair*: Vain Tales – No. DCCXVI - A Story Of The Ascot Stakes [ss] (pp. 789-791).
July.	*The Windsor Magazine*: Chronicles In Cartoon – VIII. Cricket (with Home Gordon) [ar] (pp. 157-178).

4th July.	*Vanity Fair*: Vain Tales – No. DCCXXVIII - In Which A Hero Of Henley Suffers Adversity [ss] (pp. 18-19).
11th July.	*Vanity Fair*: Vain Tales – No. DCCXXIX - How Inspector Bullen Respected The Ends Of Justice [ss] (pp. 51-52).
25th July.	*Vanity Fair*: Vain Tales – No. DCCXXXI - The Moth [ss] (pp. 115-116).
August.	*The Windsor Magazine*: Chronicles In Cartoon – IX. Rowing, Games, and Athletics [ar] (pp. 279-296).
22nd August.	*Vanity Fair*: Vain Tales – No. DCCXXXV - The Inadvisability Of Laying Your Cards On The Table [ss] (p. 244).
29th August.	*Vanity Fair*: Vain Tales – No. DCCXXXVI - The Major And The Lady [ss] (pp. 275-276).
September.	*The Windsor Magazine*: Chronicles In Cartoon – X. Empire-Builders [ar] (pp. 401-420).
5th September.	*Vanity Fair*: Vain Tales – No. DCCXXXVII - The First Case Of Dr. Edwin Maples [ss] (pp. 306-307).
12th September.	*Vanity Fair*: Vain Tales – No. DCCXXXVIII – "Dreams And Visions" – A Racing Story [ss] (pp. 339-340).
19th September.	*Vanity Fair:* The Gospel of Recreation – The Good Advice In

	The Speech of James Crichton Browne [ar] (pp. 367-368).
26th September.	*Vanity Fair*: Vain Tales – No. DCCXL - The Thirteenth Stone [ss] (pp. 404-405).
October.	*The Windsor Magazine*: Chronicles In Cartoon – XI. Science And Medicine (with Charles R. Hewitt) [ar] (pp. 539-560).
3rd October.	*Vanity Fair*: Vain Tales – No. DCCXLI - The Misfortunes Of William Henry Eagles, J.P. [ss] (pp. 437-438).
10th October.	*Vanity Fair*: Vain Tales – No. DCCXLII - A Dramatic Engagement [ss] (pp. 467-468).
17th October.	*Vanity Fair*: An Over-Married Man [pm] (p. 498).
17th October.	*Vanity Fair*: Vain Tales – No. DCCXLIII - Two Soft Things [ss] (pp. 501-503).
24th October.	*Vanity Fair*: The Gathering of the Government, Or, How They Loved Each Other [pl] (pp. 529-530).
November.	*The Windsor Magazine*: Chronicles In Cartoon – XII. Explorers And Inventors [ar] (pp. 645-660).

1907:

January.	*Appleton's Magazine* (U.S.): How Mr Denis O'Halloran Transgressed His Code [ss] (pp. 16-20).

May.	*Munsey's Magazine* (U.S): People Much Talked About in London [ar] (Vol. XXXVII, No. II, pp. 135-145).
4th May.	*The Penny Magazine*: Addington Peace of the "Yard" – I. The Terror In The Snow [ss] (pp. 145-153).
11th May.	*The Penny Magazine*: Addington Peace of the "Yard" – II. Mr Taubery's Diamond [ss] (pp. 215-222).
18th May.	*The Penny Magazine*: Addington Peace of the "Yard" – III. Mr Coran's Election [ss] (pp. 277-284).
25th May.	*The Penny Magazine*: Addington Peace of the "Yard" – IV. The Mystery Of The Causeway [ss] (pp. 340-347).
1st June.	*The Penny Magazine*: Addington Peace of the "Yard" – V. The Vanished Millionaire [ss] (pp. 408-415).
8th June.	*The Penny Magazine*: Addington Peace of the "Yard" – VI. The Mystery Of The Jade Spear [ss] (pp. 471-479).

1928:

March.	*Secret Service Stories*: Addington Peace of the "Yard" – The Vanished Billionaire [ss] (pp. 5-16).

BERTRAM FLETCHER ROBINSON

June.   *Secret Service Stories*: The Return of
                        Oliver Manton [ss] (pp. 121-126).

1936:

December.   *The Witch's Tales*: The Return of
                        Oliver Manton – A Tragic Sequence
                        to a Spiritualistic Séance [ss] (Vol. 1,
                        No. 2, pp. 52-55).

1973:

July.   *Mike Shayne Mystery Magazine*: The
                        Vanished Billionaire [ss] (Vol. 33,
                        No. 2, pp. 69-85).

1998:

Oxford University Press republished '*Fogbound*' by BFR
and J. Malcolm Fraser in a compendium of short stories
entitled *Twelve Tales of Murder* pp. 36-49 (edited by Jack
Adrian).

The Battered Silicon Dispatch Box also republished both
The Trail of the Dead by BFR and J.M. Fraser and *The
Chronicles of Addington Peace* by BFR, as a single volume.

BERTRAM FLETCHER ROBINSON

Selected Bibliography

The following sources were used in addition to those already listed in Chapter 12. Whilst every effort has been made to follow standard conventions for citation, this has not always proved possible. For example, the authors have consulted various Last Will and Testaments, birth certificates, marriage certificates, death certificates and English Census records. Such documents do not readily lend themselves to listing and in any case, each is available from either *Ancestry.com* or the General Register Office. In other cases, some 19th Century texts do not list the name of the author or authors and provide only partial details about the publisher. For these reasons the authors have either omitted partial entries from this Selected Bibliography or listed them with explanatory notes in square brackets. They have also elected to omit references to on-line sources. This decision was taken in order to preserve clarity, conserve space and because websites are transient in nature.

Andrews, C., 'The Bound of the Astorbilts' in *The Bookman*, Vol. 15, No. 4, June 1902, (New York: Dodd, Mead & Co., Publishers, 1895-1933).

Anon., 'A Devon Coachman Whose Name Has Become Immortal', *The Western Times and Gazette*, 1st November 1957 [article about Henry Baskerville].

Anon., 'A Few Copies of the Famous "Vanity Fair" Caricature of the Late...Sir Henry Irving', *The Times*, 17th October 1905, p. 10 [advertisement].

Anon., 'Ashburton Funeral – The Late Mrs. A. Baskerville', *Mid-Devon Advertiser*, 2nd June 1951.

Anon., 'Baskerville is Dead – Conan Doyle Used His Name for Sherlock Holmes Story', *The New York Times*, USA, 2nd April 1962.

Anon., 'Benefits Fiddle Prison Warning', *Herald Express* (Newton Abbot & Teignmouth Edition), 7th August 1996 [article about Rodger Garrick-Steele].

Anon., 'B.F.R.', *Daily Express*, 22nd January 1907 [obituary].

Anon., 'Coachman was in at Birth of Baskerville Tale', *Western Evening Herald*, 29th March 1962 [Henry Baskerville obituary].

Anon., *Blackheath Football Club Records 1875-1898*, (unpublished, n.d.) [This club was later renamed Blackheath Rugby Club].

Anon., 'Dartmoor in Story', *The Western Morning News*, 2nd March 1931.

Anon., 'Death of Mr. B. F. Robinson', *Mid-Devon and Newton Times*, 26th January 1907.

Anon., 'Death of Mr. B. F. Robinson', *Vanity Fair*, January 1907.

Anon., *Edinburgh Wanderers Football Club Centenary 1868 – 1968*, (self-published: 1968).

Anon., 'Festival Sports at Forde Park School', *Mid-Devon Advertiser*, 14th June 1951.

Anon., 'Football. Rugby Union Rules. London, Western, and Midland Counties v. Oxford and Cambridge', *The Times*, 10th November 1892.

Anon., 'Football. Rugby Union Rules. London, Western, and Midland Counties v. Oxford and Cambridge', *The Times*, 9th November 1893.

Anon., 'Football. Rugby Union Rules. Oxford v. Cambridge', *The Times*, 17th December 1892.

Anon., 'Football. Rugby Union Rules. Oxford v. Cambridge', *The Times*, 14th December 1893.

Anon., 'Golden Wedding Celebration – Ashburton Couple', *Western Evening Herald*, 21st November 1944 [Henry Baskerville article].

Anon., 'Henley Royal Regatta', *The Times*, 6th July 1892.

Anon., 'Henley Royal Regatta', *The Times*, 8th July 1892.

Anon., 'Henry Mathews Baskerville', *Devon Record Office*, 2005 [report for Spiring, P].

Anon., 'His Name has Gone Down in Mystery – Harry Baskerville', *South Devon Journal*, 17th October 1951.

Anon., 'Hound of the Baskervilles' – Harry Baskerville Dead; Conan Doyle Used Name', *New York Herald Tribune*, USA, 2nd April 1962.

Anon., 'In Memoriam', *The World*, 22nd January 1907 [BFR obituary].

Anon., *Ipplepen Cricket Club 1890 – 1990*, (self-published: 1990).

Anon., 'Late Mr. B. Fletcher Robinson – Funeral at Ipplepen', *The Western Morning News*, 25th January 1907.

Anon., 'Linked to the Hound of the Baskervilles', *Dawlish Post*, 15th November 1991 [article about Park Hill House in Ipplepen, a former BFR residence].

Anon., 'London Editor's Death – Mr. B. Fletcher Robinson Succumbs to Typhoid Fever', *The Western Guardian*, 24th January 1907.

Anon., 'Marriages – Robinson : Morris', *The Times*, 5th June 1902.

Anon., 'Mr. Baskerville Returned to see Old Village Friends', *The South Devon Journal*, 13th June 1951.

Anon., 'Mr. Fletcher Robinson – Memorial Service at St. Clement Danes', *Daily Express*, 26th January 1907.

Anon., 'Mr. Phil Morris, A.R.A.', *The Times*, 24th April 1902.

Anon., 'Obituary – Mr. B. Fletcher Robinson', *The Times*, 22nd January 1907.

Anon., 'Obituary – Sir John R. Robinson', *The Times*, 2nd December 1903.

Anon., 'Park Hill House in Ipplepen', *Devon Record Office*, 2005 [report for Spiring, P].

Anon., 'Pearson's New ½D. Morning Paper: Daily Express.', *The Times*, 23rd April 1900, p. 12, [adverisement].

Anon., 'Public Health', *The Times*, 2nd, 9th, 16th and 23rd January 1907 [epidemiology articles].

Anon., 'Rowing. The University Boat Race', *The Times*, 12th February 1894.

Anon., 'Sidelights on Great Crime Stories (No 10) – 'Ghost Hound" of the Marshes – Was it the Inspiration of Conan Doyle's Story?' *The Evening News*, 25th May 1939.

Anon., 'Some Gossip of the Week', *The Sphere*, 26th January 1907 [BFR obituary].

Anon., 'The Original Baskerville Dies, Aged 91', *The Western Morning News*, 30th March 1962.

Anon., 'University Intelligence', *The Times*, 26th November 1897 [BFR awarded an M.A. degree].

Anon., 'Where Sir Arthur Played Billiards', *Dawlish Post,* n.d. [article about Park Hill House].

Bath, E.J., *Newton Abbot Roundabout*, self-published, 1984 [Newton Abbot Library].

Bainbridge, J., *Newton Abbot: A History and Celebration of the Town*, (Teffont, Salisbury: Frith 2004).

Baskerville, H.M., 'A letter to the Editor [Noel Vinson]', *The Western Morning News*, February 1949. [This letter, dated 9th February 1949, was published 16th February

1949. It was written in response to a letter from H.G. Michelmore that appeared in the same newspaper on 2nd February 1949. Baskerville recalls his 1901 trip to Dartmoor with BFR and ACD. He also mentions that BFR gave him an inscribed book edition of *The Hound of the Baskervilles*].

Bigelow, S.T., 'The Singular Case of Fletcher Robinson', *The Baker Gasogene,* Vol. 1, No. 2, USA, 1961.

Budd, A.J. et al. (Marshall F., ed.), *Football: The Rugby Union Game*, (Cassell & Company Limited, 1892).

Carr, J.D., *The Life of Sir Arthur Conan Doyle*, (London: John Murray 1949).

Carter, P., *Newton Abbot*, (Exeter: The Mint Press, 2004).

Casey, P., *Clifton Rugby Football Club History*, at http://www.cliftonrfchistory.co.uk.

Cooke, H.R., 'A letter to the Editor [Noel Vinson]', *The Western Morning News*, 1949 [this letter is dated 7th February 1949 and was published 14th February 1949 in response to a letter by H. G. Michelmore that appeared in the same newspaper on 2nd February 1949. The Revd H. Cooke was the son of The Revd R.D. Cooke who had accompanied BFR on a research trip to Dartmoor in 1901. Shortly afterwards, BFR visited Dartmoor with ACD].

Cooke, R.D., *The Churches and Parishes of Ipplepen and Torbryan*, c.1930. [This article appears to have been published as a supplement to *Ipplepen Parish Magazine*].

Cramer, W.S., 'The Enigmatic B. Fletcher Robinson and the Writing of The Hound of the Baskervilles', *The Armchair Detective*, USA, Vol. 26, No. 4. (New York: The Mysterious Press, Autumn 1991).

Cresswell, B.F., *Dartmoor with its Surroundings*, (London: The Homeland Association, n.d.).

BERTRAM FLETCHER ROBINSON

Crossing, W., *Princetown – Its Rise and Progress*, (Brixham, Devon: Quay Publications, 1989).

Dam, H.J.W., 'Arthur Conan Doyle: An Appreciation of the Author of "Sir Nigel," the Great Romance Which Begins Next Sunday', *New York Tribune Sunday Magazine*, USA, 26th November 1905.

Doyle, A.C., *Memories and Adventures*, (London: Greenhill Books, 1988 [facsimile of edition published London: Hodder & Stoughton, 1924].

Doyle, A.C., 'My First Experiences in Practice', *The Strand Magazine*, Vol. 66, No. 395, November 1923.

Doyle, A.C., *The Adventure of the Norwood Builder*, Collier's Weekly Magazine, October 1903.

Doyle, A.C., *The Hound of the Baskervilles*, (London: George Newnes, Limited, 1902).

Doyle, A.C., *The Stark Munro Letters*, (London: Longmans, Green & Co., 1895).

Duncan, A., *Eliminate the Impossible: An Examination of the World of Sherlock Holmes on Page and Screen*, (Stanstead Abbotts: MX Publishing Ltd., 2008).

Duncan, S., 'The London Residences of BFR', *British Library*, 2005 [report for Spiring, P].

Duncan, S., 'BFR and The Isthmian Library', *British Library*, 2006 [report for Spiring, P].

Edwards, O.D., *The Quest for Sherlock Holmes*, (Edinburgh: Mainstream Publishing, 1983).

Evans, P., 'The Mystery of Baskerville', *Daily Express*, 16th March 1959.

Fawcett, P. H., *Exploration Fawcett*, (London: Hutchinson, 1953).

French, A., *Ipplepen*, (Exeter: Obelisk, 2003).

Garrick-Steele, R., *The House of the Baskervilles*, (London: 1st Books Library, 2003).

BERTRAM FLETCHER ROBINSON

Gillies, S., 'Published Articles by-lined by B. Fletcher Robinson in the *Daily Express*', April 1900 – July 1904", *British Library*, 2005 - 2006 [series of 17 reports for Spiring, P].

Green, R.L., 'Bertram Fletcher Robinson: An Old and Valued Friend – The Adventure of the Two Collaborators' in Purves, S. (ed.), *Hound and Horse, A Dartmoor Commonplace Book*, (The Sherlock Holmes Society of London, 1992).

Green, R.L., 'Conan Doyle and his Cricket' in Black, M.C. (ed.), *The Victorian Cricket Match – The Sherlock Holmes Society versus the PG Wodehouse Society*, (The Sherlock Holmes Society of London, 2001).

Green, R.L., 'The Hound of the Baskervilles, Part 1', *The Journal of the Sherlock Holmes Society of London*, Vol. 25, No. 3. (London: Sherlock Holmes Society 2001).

Green, R.L., 'The Hound of the Baskervilles, Part 2', *The Journal of the Sherlock Holmes Society of London*, Vol. 25, No. 4. (London: Sherlock Holmes Society 2002).

Hammond, D., *The Club: Life and Times of Blackheath F.C.*, (London: MacAitch, 1999).

Hands, S. & Webb, P., *The Book of Ashburton – Pictorial History of a Dartmoor Stannary Town*, (Tiverton: Halsgrove House, 2004).

Harrison, M., *A Study in Surmise,* (Bloomington, Indiana: Gaslight Publications 1984).

Jones, K.I., *The Mythology of The Hound of the Baskervilles*, 2nd edition, (Penzance: Oakmagic Publications, 1996).

Kelly's Directory of Devonshire, (London: Kelly's Directories Ltd, 1878/79 and 1910 [Ipplepen entries].

Klinefelter, W., *Origins of Sherlock Holmes*, (Bloomington, Indiana: Gaslight Publications 1983).

Lellenberg, J., Stashower, D. & Foley, C., *Arthur Conan Doyle: A Life in Letters*, (London: HarperPress, 2007).

Lycett, A., *Conan Doyle: The Man Who Created Sherlock Holmes*, (London: Weidenfeld & Nicolson, 2007).

Marshall, A., *Out and About – Random Reminiscences*, (London: John Murray, 1933).

Marshall, H. (with J.P. Jordan), *Oxford v. Cambridge: The Story of the University Rugby Match*, (London: Clerke & Cockeran, 1951).

Matson, C.G., 'Automobile Topics: The Paris Automobile Show', *The World*, 11th December 1906 [BFR was editor of this newspaper at the time of his death. According to various sources he contracted typhoid whilst visiting the Paris Automobile Exhibition during December 1906].

Matson, C.G., 'Automobile Topics: The Paris Automobile Show', *The World*, 18th December 1906.

Matson, C.G., 'Automobile Topics: The Paris Automobile Show', *The World*, 25th December 1906.

McClure, M.W., 'Myth-Conception Regarding The Hound of the Baskervilles', *The Devonshire Chronicle, The Quarterly Journal of The Chester Baskerville Society*, Vol. 2, No. 2, (Illinois: The Chester Baskerville Society, 1989).

McNabb, J., *My Friend, Mr. Fletcher Robinson*, (unpublished & supplied by author, c.1985).

McNabb, J., 'The Curious Incident of the Hound on Dartmoor' in *Occasional Papers No 1, - Bootmakers of Toronto*, (Toronto: Bootmakers of Toronto, 1984).

Michelmore, H.G., *A letter to Henry Baskerville*, unpublished, 8th February 1949 [written in response to a letter received and dated 7th February 1949. Michelmore was BFR's friend for more than 20 years and acted as solicitor to the Robinson family from about 1900–1946].

Michelmore, H.G., *A letter to the Editor* [Noel Vinson], *The Western Morning News*, 1949 [dated 2nd February 1949 and published 7th February 1949, shortly after a review about Dickson Carr's *The Life of Sir Arthur Conan Doyle* appeared in the same newspaper].

Michelmore, H.G., *A letter to Miss Mary Taylor*, dated 30th January 1907 [this letter records H.G. Michelmore's reaction to the recent news of the death of BFR and also outlines his arrangements for travelling to London to settle the estate. This item is held by the British Library of Political and Economic Science ref. Mill-Taylor, Vol. 29, No. 307].

Michelmore, H.G., *Fishing Facts and Fancies*, (Exeter: A. Wheaton & Co., 1946).

Old Cliftonian Society, *Clifton College Register 1862 - 1947*, (Old Cliftonian Society, 1947).

Pemberton, M., *Sixty Years Ago and After*, (London: Hutchinson & Co., 1936).

Pugh, B.W., *A Chronology of the Life of Sir Arthur Conan Doyle – New Revised and Expanded Edition*, (self-published [2nd edition], 2003).

Pugh, B.W., Spiring, P.R. & Weller, P.L., *Bertram Fletcher Robinson: An Annotated and Analytical Chronology and Bibliography*, (http://www.bfronline.biz/).

Pugh, B.W. & Spiring, P.R., *On the Trail of Sir Arthur Conan Doyle: An Illustrated Devon Tour*, (Brighton: Book Guild Publishing, 2008).

Quiller-Couch, A., *Memories and Opinions*, (Cambridge University Press, 1944).

Rice, F.A., (compiler), *The Granta and its Contributors 1889-1914*, (London: Constable & Co. Ltd., 1924).

Robinson, J.R., *Fifty Years on Fleet Street*, (London: MacMillan & Company Limited, 1904).

Ruber, P.A., 'Sir Arthur Conan Doyle & Fletcher Robinson: an Epitaph', *The Baker Street Gasogene*, Vol. 1, No 2, New York).

Saville, G., 'The War of the Baskervilles', *The Independent* 11th July 2001.

Sladen, D. B. W., *Twenty Years of My Life*, (New York: E.P. Dutton & Co. Publishers, 1913).

Stashower, D., *Teller of Tales: The Life of Arthur Conan Doyle*, (New York: Henry Holt & Co., 1999).

The Chanticleer, (Foakes-Jackson, J. ed. & others), J. Palmer, No 16-28, 1890-1894 [Jesus College magazine that changed its name to *The Chanticlere* from October 1892].

The Medical Directory, 1870-1905, (London: Churchill Livingston).

The Newtonian, (Newton Abbot: G.H. Hearder, Vol. 6-14, 1881-1890 [Newton College magazine edited by B. Fletcher Robinson between 1887 and 1889].

Weller, P.L., 'Deposits in the Vault: Together Again on the Moor?', *Stimson & Co Gazette*, No. 3, (USA: 1992).

Weller, P.L., *Terror In The Snow by Bertram Fletcher Robinson, An Annotated Text*, (Hampshire: Sherlock Publications, 1995).

Weller, P.L., *The Hound of the Baskervilles – Hunting the Dartmoor Legend*, (Tiverton: Devon Books, 2001).

Wheeler, E., '"Rescuer' of Sherlock Holmes', *The Western Morning News*, 24th October. 1969.

White, W., *History Gazetteer & Directory of Devonshire* (Sheffield: Robert Leader, 1850) [entries on Ipplepen].

Williams, J.E.H., 'The Reader: Arthur Conan Doyle', *The Bookman*, (USA, April 1902).

Willmoth, F., *BFR and Dr. Henry Menzies*, (Jesus College, The University of Cambridge, 2005 [report for Spiring, P].

BERTRAM FLETCHER ROBINSON

Wright, N., & Ashford, D., 'Sir Arthur Conan Doyle's 'The Hound of the Baskervilles'', in *Book and Magazine Collector*, March 2002 No. 216, (London: Diamond Publishing Group Ltd., 2002).

Zunic, J., 'Origins of the Hound 1: Bertie and Max", *The Northumberland Gazette*, November 1989.

The Authors

Paul R. Spiring (left) and Brian W. Pugh (right) together with the actor
Edward Hardwicke who played Dr. Watson alongside the late Jeremy
Brett as Sherlock Holmes.

Brian W. Pugh lives in Lewes, East Sussex not far from the
town of Crowborough (the home of Sir Arthur Conan
Doyle 1907-1930). He was born in 1944 and has lived in
Lewes all of his life. Brian worked for British Gas as a
Supervisor and Assessor for 30 years and is now semi-
retired. He first became interested in Sherlock Holmes in
1958 when he received his first Holmes book *The Complete
Short Stories*.

Brian is Curator of The Conan Doyle (Crowborough)
Establishment, a society dedicated to Arthur Conan Doyle;
and is responsible for maintaining the modest collection of
Conan Doyle ephemera that is owned by that society. He is
also a member of numerous other societies including The
Sherlock Holmes Society of London, The Sydney
Passengers and The Poor Folks upon the Moors. Brian has

published many items pertaining to Conan Doyle and is frequently consulted by the media and others on this subject.

Paul R. Spiring lives in Karlsruhe in Germany. He was born in Barrow-in-Furness in 1968 and has lived in Scotland, the West of England, Wales and The Netherlands. He was previously employed by both the Police and Fire Services but has now been teaching for 13 years. Paul's interest in Sherlock Holmes was stimulated by the Basil Rathbone films that he first saw as a child living in Devon.

Paul is both a Chartered Biologist and Physicist and is currently employed by the Department for Education as Head of Biology at the European School of Karlsruhe. He is the author of a website called *BFRonline.BIZ* that commemorates the memory of Bertram Fletcher Robinson. Paul is also a member of The Conan Doyle (Crowborough) Establishment, The Sherlock Holmes Society of London and The Sydney Passengers'.

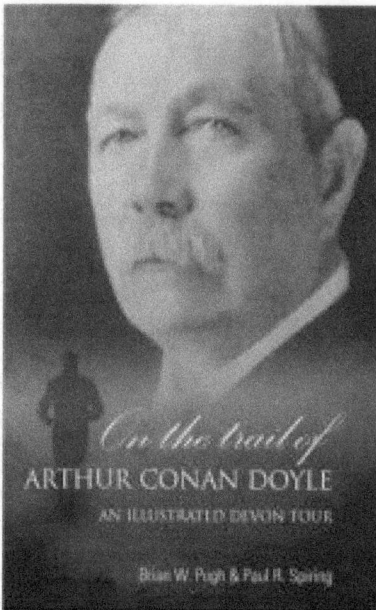

Also by Brian Pugh and Paul Spiring

On the Trail of
Arthur Conan Doyle

An Illustrated Devon Tour

235

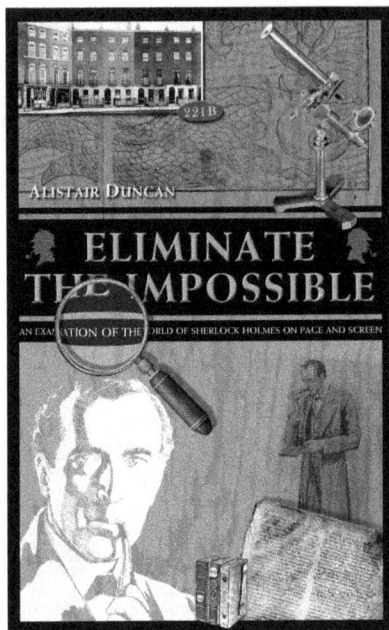

Also from MX Publishing, by Alistair Duncan

Eliminate the Impossible

An Examination of the World of
Sherlock Holmes on Page and Screen

www.ingramcontent.com/pod-product-compliance
Lightning Source LLC
Chambersburg PA
CBHW060305100426
42742CB00011B/1873